1996 COMMEMORATIVE STAMP COLLECTION

TABLE OF CONTENTS

UTAH STATEHOOD	WINTER GARDEN FLOWERS	ERNEST E. JUST	SMITHSONIAN	LUNAR NEW YEAR	PIONEERS OF COMMUNICATION
SALT LAKE CITY, UT JANUARY 4	KENNETT SQUARE, PA JANUARY 19	WASHINGTON, DC FEBRUARY 1	WASHINGTON, DC FEBRUARY 7	SAN FRANCISCO, CA FEBRUARY 8	NEW YORK, NY FEBRUARY 22
McRAY MAGLEBY PROVO, UT	NED SEIDLER HAMPTON BAY, NY	DICK SHEAFF NORWOOD, MA	TOM ENGEMAN CARBONDALE, CO	CLARENCE LEE HONOLULU, HI	FRED OTNES WEST REDDING, CT

"Not wanting to feature anything with political or religious overtones, I chose one of Utah's natural wonders as my subject."

"The winter flowers are all tiny—you really have to come up close to see them. For the stamp, they were maximized."

"This is the first stamp in a reconfigured Black Heritage series; while earlier issues had emphasized graphic formats, the new intention is to bring each person strongly to the fore."

"I collected stamps as a child, and they were my first introduction to what graphic design could be—and here I am designing stamps."

"I have been enriched by discovering the art and culture of my Chinese heritage."

"It was very interesting to work on stamps paying tribute to four individuals who were great contributors to the field in which I work."

20   22   24   26   28   30   32

FULBRIGHT SCHOLARSHIPS	MARATHON	OLYMPIC CLASSIC COLLECTION	GEORGIA O'KEEFFE	TENNESSEE STATEHOOD	AMERICAN INDIAN DANCES	PREHISTORIC ANIMALS
FAYETTEVILLE, AR FEBRUARY 28	BOSTON, MA APRIL 11	WASHINGTON, DC MAY 2	SANTA FE, NM MAY 23	NASHVILLE, TN MAY 31	OKLAHOMA CITY, OK JUNE 7	TORONTO, CANADA JUNE 8
DICK SHEAFF NORWOOD, MA	MICHAEL BARTALOS SAN FRANCISCO, CA	RICHARD WALDREP SPARKS, MD	MARGARET BAUER WASHINGTON, DC	PHIL JORDAN FALLS CHURCH, VA	KEITH BIRDSONG MUSKOGEE, OK	DAVIS MELTZER HUNTINGDON VALLEY, PA

"This design hopes to suggest the human intellect applied in an international arena."

"A close look reveals the marathoner sporting a pair of winged feet, an allusion to the fleet-footed Greek god Hermes and the marathon's Hellenic origins."

"I see stamps as miniature posters, or even billboards. In these, I tried to say something about the Olympic Games."

"I spent a lot of time looking through all of O'Keeffe's flowers, and the red poppy is my favorite."

"The unique beauty of the Capitol and the power of the sculpture are shown in Robin Hood's photograph, expressing the spirit of this milestone Tennessee anniversary."

"Though I'm less than one-quarter Indian, I've always been proud of my Indian heritage, so I was very pleased to do this stamp."

"About two years before beginning work on these stamps, I ordered a replica of a Smilodon skull, which turned out to be prophetic."

BREAST CANCER AWARENESS	JAMES DEAN	FOLK HEROES	OLYMPIC ANNIVERSARY SHEET	IOWA STATEHOOD	RURAL FREE DELIVERY	RIVERBOATS
WASHINGTON, DC JUNE 15	BURBANK, CA JUNE 24	ANAHEIM, CA JULY 11	ATLANTA, GA JULY 19	DUBUQUE, IA AUGUST 1	CHARLESTON, WV AUGUST 7	ORLANDO, FL AUGUST 22

TOM MANN
WARRENTON, VA

"Working on issue-related stamps such as this one is what I find most fulfilling and enjoyable, because they are educational."

MICHAEL DEAS
NEW YORK, NY

"The grassy fields evoke Indiana, where Dean was born, and the California fields where he died. The stormy sky refers to the turbulent nature of the characters he portrayed."

DAVE LA FLEUR
DERBY, KS

"The challenge of a stamp is to create a powerful composition within Lilliputian dimensions. Folk heroes add an ironic twist—larger-than-life figures squeezed into a tiny rectangle."

CARL HERRMAN
PONTE VEDRA BEACH, FL

"It was fun doing my first nude stamp."

CARL HERRMAN
PONTE VEDRA BEACH, FL

"This was the first time I ever worked with a deceased illustrator. This image is from a painting by Grant Wood. Mr. Wood was no problem at all."

DICK SHEAFF
NORWOOD, MA

"A rural carrier in a rural scene, then and now."

DEAN ELLIS
AMAGANSETT, NY

"While the riverboats in this series were selected by marine historians, I suggested that the stamps reflect the geographic localities in which they operated."

48   50   52   54   56   58   60

BIG BAND LEADERS

NEW YORK, NY
SEPTEMBER 11

BILL NELSON
RICHMOND, VA

"The portrait photography of the golden age has always intrigued and inspired me with its use of light and drama; it was a joy to recreate it for the unique medium of the stamp."

SONGWRITERS

NEW YORK, NY
SEPTEMBER 11

GREGG RUDD
FAIRFIELD, CT

"I appreciate the music of these composers. They came out of a more innocent, naive time, yet their music helped people escape from the harsh realities of the Depression and World War II."

F. SCOTT FITZGERALD

ST. PAUL, MN
SEPTEMBER 27

MICHAEL DEAS
NEW YORK, NY

"The likeness is based on a well-known photograph of Fitzgerald taken in the early 1920s. The background is meant to evoke the setting of The Great Gatsby."

ENDANGERED SPECIES

SAN DIEGO, CA
OCTOBER 2

JAMES BALOG
BOULDER, CO

"I'm trying to visually reflect the loss of habitat and alienation of these animals in contemporary civilization."

COMPUTER TECHNOLOGY

PHILADELPHIA, PA
OCTOBER 9

NANCY SKOLOS
AND TOM WEDELL
BOSTON, MA

"The whole idea was to photographically represent the computer as an extension of the human mind."

DECEMBER HOLIDAYS

CONTEMPORARY HOLIDAY
NORTH POLE, AK
OCTOBER 9

HOLIDAY CELEBRATION
(Hanukkah)
WASHINGTON, DC
OCTOBER 22

TRADITIONAL HOLIDAY
(Christmas)
RICHMOND, VA
NOVEMBER 1

JULIA TALCOTT
NEWTON, MA
(Contemporary)

"This was a very easy subject for me to do because it has to do with my life as it is right now."

HANNAH SMOTRICH
WASHINGTON, DC
(Holiday Celebration)

"The choice of the bright colors, playful angles, and irregular shape was meant to convey the joyful nature of the holiday."

DICK SHEAFF
NORWOOD, MA
(Traditional)

"A detail from Paolo de Matteis' early-18th-century painting gives us a particularly warm and engaging Madonna and Child."

CYCLING

NEW YORK, NY
NOVEMBER 1

MCRAY MAGLEBY
PROVO, UT

"I wanted to capture the feeling of the speed and excitement of an actual high-performance road race."

Introduction

Proverbial wisdom says a picture is worth a thousand words. Perhaps this is never truer than when the picture in question is a 1996 United States commemorative postage stamp.

This year's commemorative stamps offer something for everyone. Lovers of literature and the arts, gardeners, animal lovers, and sports fans will all have their own favorites. History buffs are sure to find the subjects represented on this year's commemorative stamps a fascinating assortment.

There are stamps honoring art and artists—painter Georgia O'Keeffe, writer F. Scott Fitzgerald, American Indian dances, big band leaders, popular songwriters, actor James Dean—and scientists, including the great black American research scientist and professor Ernest E. Just. Four 19th-century inventors whose work helped usher in the information age are represented here, as are 15 endangered animal species. The Smithsonian Institution's 150th anniversary is celebrated, and so are milestone statehood anniversaries of Tennessee, Iowa, and Utah. The Rural Free Delivery program is honored on its centennial, and the Modern Olympic Games are honored on theirs.

This is just a hint of the variety to be found on this year's stamps. Each one opens a window to a world of its own, with its own history and stories to tell. Perhaps the single stamp most emblematic of the entire group is the one honoring the world of learning supported by the Fulbright program, observing its 50th anniversary this year.

The fascinating stories behind these stamps—many of which are told in the following pages—can only begin to suggest their appeal. Each stamp is a piece of Americana, a concentrated bit of history. For an object to pack so much information into such a small frame, and to be beautiful on top of it all, is to enter the realm of marvel and magic.

Like all good magic tricks, stamps leave us wondering how, exactly, they work—how do they pack so many stories into such a small space? Part of the answer is in the painstaking planning and work that goes on behind the scenes at the U. S. Postal Service. The statements by the stamp designers included in the table of contents provide a brief glance at this "backstage" work.

Without further delay, we invite you to embark on a journey, simply by turning the page. You're sure to be intrigued, delighted, and charmed.

This page (clockwise from top): 1925 Boston Marathon; American Indian Traditional dancer; breast cancer support group. Various 1996 commemorative stamps are also shown. Opposite page: Georgia O'Keeffe, photographed by Alfred Stieglitz, 1922.

One of Utah's most prominent landmarks is the Great Salt Lake. Formed from prehistoric Lake Bonneville, it is the largest inland body of salt water in the Western Hemisphere. Its size has fluctuated from 2,500 square miles in 1873 to 900 square miles in 1963. The lake's unique ecosystem supports hundreds of shore and migratory birds, many of them at the world-famous Bear River Bird Refuge. Several islands dot the lake. The largest, Antelope Island, is a state park with extensive recreational facilities and many species of wildlife, including a herd of 600 bison introduced over 100 years ago. The Great Salt Lake also provides Utah with unique lake industries. Over 400,000 tons of table salt are produced from minerals found in the lake each year, and a flourishing brine shrimp industry annually contributes $30 million to the state's economy.

Place stamp here

Utah Statehood

U*tah, We Love Thee*
—UTAH STATE SONG

Utah was named for the Ute Indians, one of the original Indian tribes living in the area when Spanish missionaries visited in 1776. The Ute, with their neighbors, the Bannock, Northwestern Shoshone, Southern Paiute, Gosiute, and Navajo, had lived and flourished in the region for several hundred years before contact with Europeans.

Utah and its native population remained relatively isolated from the newly formed United States until the Mormons came in 1847, fleeing religious persecution. According to legend, Mormon leader Brigham Young brought his party down the Wasatch Mountains and through Emigration Canyon, pointing down into the Great Salt Lake Valley, he said, "This is the place." For the Mormons, Utah was the promised land, and they set about building a community and environment worthy of that title.

The 11th largest state, Utah today has more than two million acres of national parkland. Traveling in Utah has been compared to visiting another planet every few miles: two Rocky Mountain ranges, the Wasatch and the Uinta, contrast with three deserts. Utah is the home of thousands of spectacular geologic formations. Across the southern portion of the state, rock forms natural bridges, arches, pinnacles, and fins. One formation, Capitol Dome, resembles the U. S. Capitol.

Tourism is an important source of revenue for the state. Utah's weather and landscape make it popular with many athletes, including hikers, skiers, mountain bikers, rock climbers, and river rafters. The Bonneville Salt Flats, one of the flattest, most obstacle-free places on earth, is much loved by automobile racers. For growing numbers of retirees and other urban refugees, Utah's sun, fun, low crime rate, and high employment rate still represent the promised land.

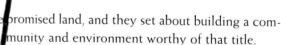

This page (clockwise from top middle): mountain climber at Indian Creek Canyon; Handcart Pioneers' First View of the Salt Lake Valley, painted in 1890 by C. C. A. Christensen; Brigham Young as territorial governor of Utah; Ute Indians; skier in Utah. Opposite page: rock spires of Silent City, Bryce Canyon National Park. Inset: salt harvest at Great Salt Lake.

Place
stamps
here

Another exquisite winter flower is the Christmas rose, a popular member of the diverse genus *Helleborus*. Starry-white flowers up to three inches across are lit from the center by golden stamens, and handsome foliage is composed of divided evergreen leaves. According to one legend, the Christmas rose flourished in Heaven's garden and was tended by angels; an anonymous poem described it as a "symbol of God's promise, care, and love."

Winter Garden Flowers

JANUARY 19, KENNETT SQUARE, PENNSYLVANIA

The flowers of late winter and early spring occupy places in our hearts well out of proportion to their size.

—GERTRUDE S. WISTER, GARDENER

Winter flowers offer us hope and encouragement by braving the cold.

One of Mother Nature's most appreciated winter gifts is the modest but charming crocus. Spotting the season's first goblet-shaped beauty rising from a lining of snow is as refreshing as seeing the first robin. The Romans revered the crocus as their symbol of life, beauty, and youth, and the Dutch honored it with years of study and cultivation, giving us an enchanting variety of sizes, colors, patterns, and fragrances.

The winter aconite, a member of the buttercup family, is prized for its golden-yellow sepals framed by a collar of bright green leaves. In rock gardens or under trees and shrubs, a covering of these showy perennials is like a streak of sunshine at a time of year when most of the landscape still looks tired and barren.

The pansy's kaleidoscopic colors range from the palest to the richest. "Pansy" is an Anglicized spelling of *pensée*, the French word for "thought;" many people see a face when they look at these flowers, which are reputed to have romantic powers and are often used for decorative and culinary purposes. The pansy so widely known today was not hybridized in earnest until Victorian times and is closely related to the smaller and cheerful Johnny-jump-up.

No other flower signals the loosening of winter's grip as early as the snowdrop. For good reason, the Victorians called it "the flower of hope." The bell-shaped blooms, sometimes likened to lampshades holding spring's first light bulbs, nod downward as if to protect themselves from winter's last storms and winds. The other name for these white beauties, *Galanthus*, comes from the Greek words for "milk" and "flower."

The *Anemone blanda*, another member of the buttercup family, is the mountain windflower of Greece, and one legend says that the blossoms would only open when the wind blew. The friendly faces of this anemone are found in the shade or semi-shade of many gardens and in the wild at high-altitude locations. The mauve, pink, blue, or white parts of this perennial flower look like petals, but they are actually sepals.

This page (clockwise from top): snowdrops; crocus; winter aconite; illustration of Crocus versicolor from Curtis' Botanical Magazine. Opposite page: pansy. Inset: Christmas rose.

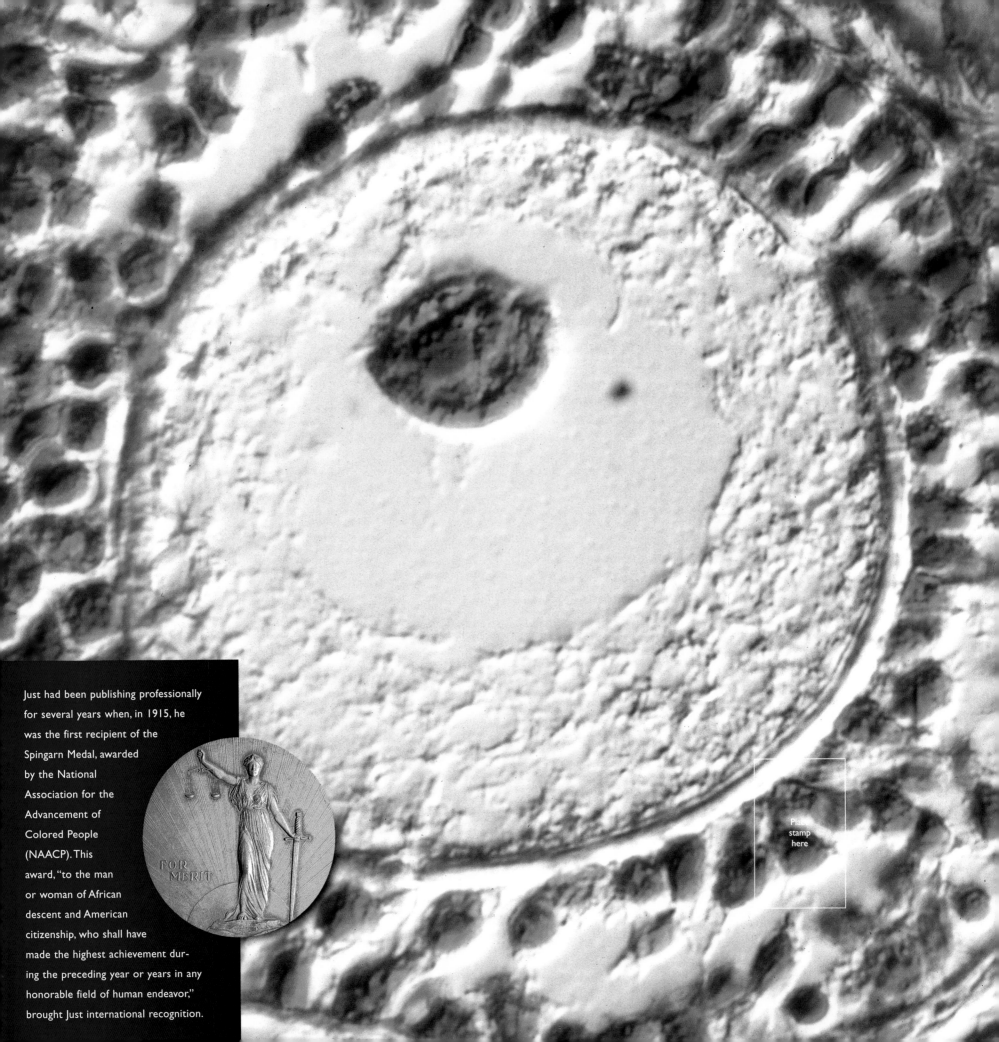

Just had been publishing professionally for several years when, in 1915, he was the first recipient of the Spingarn Medal, awarded by the National Association for the Advancement of Colored People (NAACP). This award, "to the man or woman of African descent and American citizenship, who shall have made the highest achievement during the preceding year or years in any honorable field of human endeavor," brought Just international recognition.

Place stamp here

Ernest E. Just

February 1, Washington, D.C.

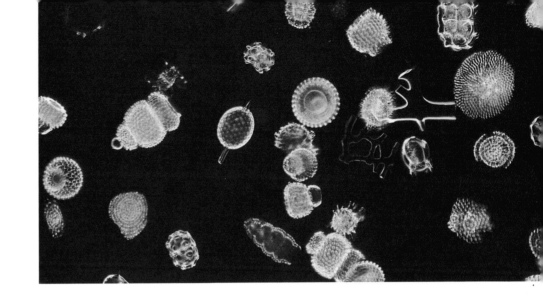

W

e feel the beauty of Nature because we are part of Nature....
—Ernest E. Just, *The Biology of the Cell Surface*

A great black American research scientist and professor, Ernest E. Just was born in Charleston, South Carolina, in 1883. He graduated *magna cum laude* from Dartmouth College in June 1907 and joined the faculty at Howard University as an instructor in English that fall.

While at Dartmouth, Just was honored for his outstanding record in biology. In the summer of 1909, Professor Frank R. Lillie, head of the zoology department at the University of Chicago, invited Just to be his research assistant at the Marine Biological Laboratory at Woods Hole, Massachusetts. Their professional relationship developed into a lifelong friendship. While working with Lillie in the summers, Just chose his three areas of specialization: fertilization, cellular physiology, and experimental embryology. Just confined his graduate work to Woods Hole in the summers and to Howard in the winters, all the while teaching a heavy schedule.

In June 1916, after a year's leave from teaching biology at Howard, Just completed his requirements and earned his Ph.D. in zoology at the University of Chicago, again graduating *magna cum laude*.

In 1920, and again in 1928, a well-known philanthropist, Julius Rosenwald, granted money to Howard University for use by Just. The terms of his second gift stipulated that Just must remain as head of the zoology department, that he stop teaching a double load, and that he be granted a six-month leave each year to pursue his research. As a result, Just now published more frequently than before.

In the 1920s and 1930s, Just was increasingly torn between his teaching duties and his desire to concentrate on research. He was one of the first Americans invited to do research at the Kaiser Wilhelm Institute for Biology in Berlin-Dahlem, considered one of the best research labs in the world at that time. Just died in 1941 in Washington, D.C., where he is buried.

This page (clockwise from top): radiolarian, microscopic marine life; the Just family, circa 1890 (left to right: Inez, Ernest, Mary, Hunter); Just at his microscope, circa 1936. Opposite page: an egg cell magnified 320 times. Inset: the NAACP's Spingarn Medal, awarded to Just in 1915.

The Castle is the most recognizable icon associated with the Smithsonian. The various towers, gables, and battlements lend obvious character, but the graceful arches and the opalescent stained-glass windows are also noteworthy. The first building erected as part of the Institution, the Castle was designed by James Renwick and constructed of sandstone between 1847 and 1855. Upon completion, the east wing became the home of Joseph Henry, the first Secretary of the Smithsonian. Today, the Castle remains one of the best-known landmarks in Washington, D.C.

Place
stamp
here

Smithsonian

To the United States of America, to found at Washington, under the name of the Smithsonian Institution, an Establishment for the increase & diffusion of knowledge among men.

—FROM THE WILL OF JAMES SMITHSON, 1826

The world's largest museum complex, the Smithsonian Institution was founded with a bequest from James Smithson, a British chemist. Smithson's will stipulated that his nephew should receive his fortune—but that if the nephew died without heirs, the money should be used to establish an educational institution in America.

In 1838, the United States received Smithson's bequest: bags of gold sovereigns, then the equivalent of $515,169. Eight years later, on August 10, 1846, President James K. Polk signed an Act of Congress establishing the Smithsonian Institution in its present form.

Today, the Smithsonian Institution is an international education and research complex, encompassing 16 museums and galleries, several research facilities, and the National Zoo. The Castle houses the Smithsonian Information Center, administrative offices, and the Woodrow Wilson International Center for Scholars, as well as James Smithson's crypt. Each Smithsonian museum has its own director and staff. The Smithsonian has about 6,700 people on its permanent staff and almost 5,000 volunteers.

The collection is estimated to comprise more than 140 million objects, including many artifacts donated by individuals; others are purchased by the Institution or arrive through other channels. Some of the treasures in the Smithsonian collection are the Apollo 14 command module, the ruby slippers worn by Judy Garland in *The Wizard of Oz*, Dizzy Gillespie's trumpet, George Washington's sword, Amelia Earhart's flight suit, Rodin's *Walking Man* sculpture, and Tecumseh's tomahawk. These objects and nearly 300 other artifacts have been shown around the country as part of the Smithsonian's sesquicentennial celebration. Artifacts not on display are stored in collection study areas and are available to researchers by appointment.

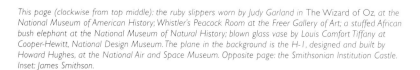

This page (clockwise from top middle): the ruby slippers worn by Judy Garland in The Wizard of Oz, *at the National Museum of American History; Whistler's Peacock Room at the Freer Gallery of Art; a stuffed African bush elephant at the National Museum of Natural History; blown glass vase by Louis Comfort Tiffany at Cooper-Hewitt, National Design Museum. The plane in the background is the H-1, designed and built by Howard Hughes, at the National Air and Space Museum. Opposite page: the Smithsonian Institution Castle. Inset: James Smithson.*

In ancient China, as in most other cultures, the New Year was celebrated as the sun's daily appearance increased in duration between the winter solstice and the coming of spring. The Chinese treated the New Year as an important holiday, a time for starting fresh. The New Year's holiday included celebrations designed to complete the old business of the passing year and prepare for the year to come—debts were paid, family hierarchy was determined, community ties were strengthened—all with the hope that these preparations would provide a firm foundation upon which to build a successful new year.

Place stamp here

Lunar New Year

FEBRUARY 8, SAN FRANCISCO, CALIFORNIA

*P*eace and togetherness in the New Year

(SHOWN IN CHINESE CHARACTERS IN BACKGROUND)

The lunar New Year begins in January or February each year, at the first new moon after the sun enters what Westerners call Aquarius. It signals the imminent arrival of spring and is celebrated in most East Asian and many Southeast Asian countries.

The Chinese lunar calendar is organized into cycles of 12 years; each year is associated with an animal emblem. According to legend, the Jade King once invited 12 animals to Heaven. The rat was the first to arrive, riding on the back of the ox, who had hoped to be first. Next in line were the tiger, rabbit, and dragon, followed by the snake, the horse, and the goat. After them came the monkey, the rooster, and the dog; the pig brought up the rear.

To show his appreciation for his guests, the Jade King named a year after each animal and declared that the years should run in the order of their arrival at his party. Further, the Jade King determined that people would inherit the characteristics of the animal of their birth year. Rats would be acquisitive and resourceful, dogs would be loyal, pigs would be hedonistic, and so on.

1996 is the Year of the Rat. In Chinese legend, the rat is associated with money. A rat is said to be "counting money" when it is heard scavenging for food at night. As might be expected, people born in the Year of the Rat are opportunistic survivors who can make it through lean times thanks to their hard work, cleverness, and ambition. Rats are social types who relish a party or a big, noisy conversation. They seldom throw anything away and often have very large families. They are escape artists who can always be counted on to find their way out of trouble, and they rarely miss anything in their environment. Some well-known "rats" are Lauren Bacall, Marlon Brando, Al Gore, Richard Nixon, William Shakespeare, and George Washington.

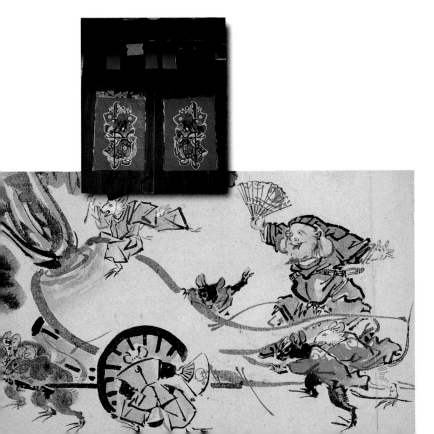

This page (clockwise from top): young girl in New Year's parade in Los Angeles; traditional New Year's Lion Dance; wood-block print of rat; Japanese painting of the god of Fortune and his messenger, the rat; New Year's decoration to ward off demons, Guangxi, China. Opposite page: lion dance costume. Inset: drummer during lion dance in Hawaii.

Place stamps here

In the last few years, communications technology has taken a direction that this quartet of inventors could not have imagined. The rise of the Internet, a global computer network, enables users to transmit digital documents—text, graphics, audio, and video—in a mere instant. The number of Internet users worldwide is difficult to know for sure, but has been estimated at more than 50 million.

Pioneers of Communication

Transport of the mails, transport of the human voice, transport of flickering pictures—in this century as in others our highest accomplishments still have the single aim of bringing men together.

—ANTOINE DE SAINT-EXUPÉRY, FRENCH WRITER

The age of worldwide communication dawned about 150 years ago, as enterprising inventors, represented by the gentlemen on these stamps, developed machines and processes that laid the foundations for efficient mass communication.

Ottmar Mergenthaler was born in Germany, where he trained as a clock- and watchmaker, but he spent most of his life in Baltimore, Maryland, dedicating himself to solving the problem of setting type by machine. He succeeded by inventing the Linotype, which dramatically reduced the amount of time and expense involved in typesetting. This led to a significant drop in the prices of newspapers, magazines, and books. The Linotype brought rapid expansion to all areas of publishing, making information and literature available to more people than ever before.

Born in England, **Eadweard Muybridge** spent many years in California, where he made photographic studies of animals and humans in motion. Using 12 to 24 cameras, Muybridge made the first successive stop-motion photographs of these subjects. The pictures were later transformed into an illusion of moving images by his zoopraxiscope, a projection machine with a hand-rotated disc onto which he had transferred the photographs. It was the first machine to project sequential, still photographs into moving pictures on a screen.

After a childhood spent on a farm in Connecticut, **Frederic E. Ives** played an important role in the development of halftone printing, still in use today. The process transfers continuous tones of a photograph to a metal plate, on which they appear as tiny dots of various sizes. The size of the dots varies with the tone. This permitted pictures to be printed from the photographic halftone printing plates, instead of from expensive, less accurate, hand-carved wood engravings, and led to the extensive use of halftone illustrations in newspapers and periodicals.

William K. L. Dickson was born in France to an English father and Scottish mother. He spent several years in the United States, mostly in the employment of Thomas Edison. They collaborated on the kinetoscope, a forerunner of the motion picture film projector. When a strip of film on vertical pulleys passed quickly between a lens and an electric light source, the viewer, while peering into a peephole and through the lens, could see glimpses of each frame. This produced short, lifelike moving pictures.

This page (clockwise from top): cover page illustration from a book by Dickson and his wife; a Mergenthaler Linotype, first machine to set type; Muybridge's zoopraxiscope. Background: enlarged dot pattern from an Ives halftone (shown on opposite page, lower left). Opposite page (clockwise from top right): a line of type set by Mergenthaler on his Linotype; Dickson's "The Sneeze"—the oldest surviving copyrighted film; an Ives halftone; a Muybridge photographic study of a horse in motion. Inset: a opening screen from an online service.

While the majority of Fulbright recipients are graduate students and scholars, participants also include many professionals from outside academia: doctors, journalists, lawyers, artists, and others. A few of the many notable Fulbright winners include United Nations Secretary-General Boutros Boutros-Ghali, graphic designer Milton Glaser, composers Aaron Copland and Philip Glass, poet Rita Dove (below), opera singer Anna Moffo, and writers Eudora Welty, Umberto Eco, and Chinua Achebe.

Place stamp here

Fulbright Scholarships

FEBRUARY 28, FAYETTEVILLE, ARKANSAS

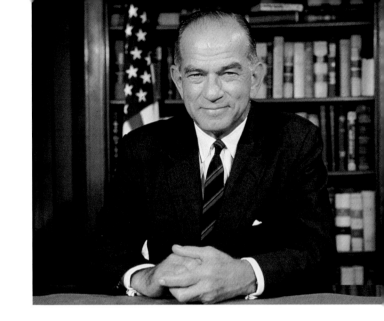

*E*ducational exchange can turn nations into people, contributing as no other form of communication can to the humanizing of international relations.

— J. WILLIAM FULBRIGHT, SPEECH TO THE COUNCIL FOR
INTERNATIONAL EDUCATION EXCHANGE, 1983

Established in 1946 under legislation introduced by Senator J. William Fulbright, the scholarship program bearing his name is designed to "increase mutual understanding and peaceful relations between the people of the United States and the people of other countries." The program is administered by the U. S. Government in cooperation with 130 countries around the world.

Annual appropriations by Congress and contributions from foreign governments and private organizations have been major sources of funding. Binational commissions, comprising equal numbers of Americans and citizens of the host country, design and operate programs that address the educational needs and resources of both countries involved.

More than 200,000 persons have received Fulbright scholarships. Slightly more than half of these individuals have come from countries outside the United States. There are several types of awards. While graduate students receive the largest number of grants, many fellowships are given to academics or professionals to lecture or conduct research abroad; the program also facilitates the exchange of teaching assignments between American and foreign educators. An overwhelming majority of former Fulbrighters say the opportunities provided by the program helped them gain a deeper understanding of their own country, as well as the country they visited.

Praising the Fulbright scholarship program in 1995 for its ability to put a human face on foreign relations, President Bill Clinton said it "has changed the whole direction of policy in country after country after country." More than 20 years earlier, noted historian Arnold Toynbee had pronounced the Fulbright program "one of the really generous and imaginative things that have been done in the world since World War II."

This page (clockwise from top): Senator J. William Fulbright, 1967; Secretary-General of the United Nations, Boutros Boutros-Ghali, Fulbright recipient; flags of many nations; composer Philip Glass, Fulbright recipient. Opposite page: Senator J. William Fulbright. Inset: poet Rita Dove, Fulbright recipient.

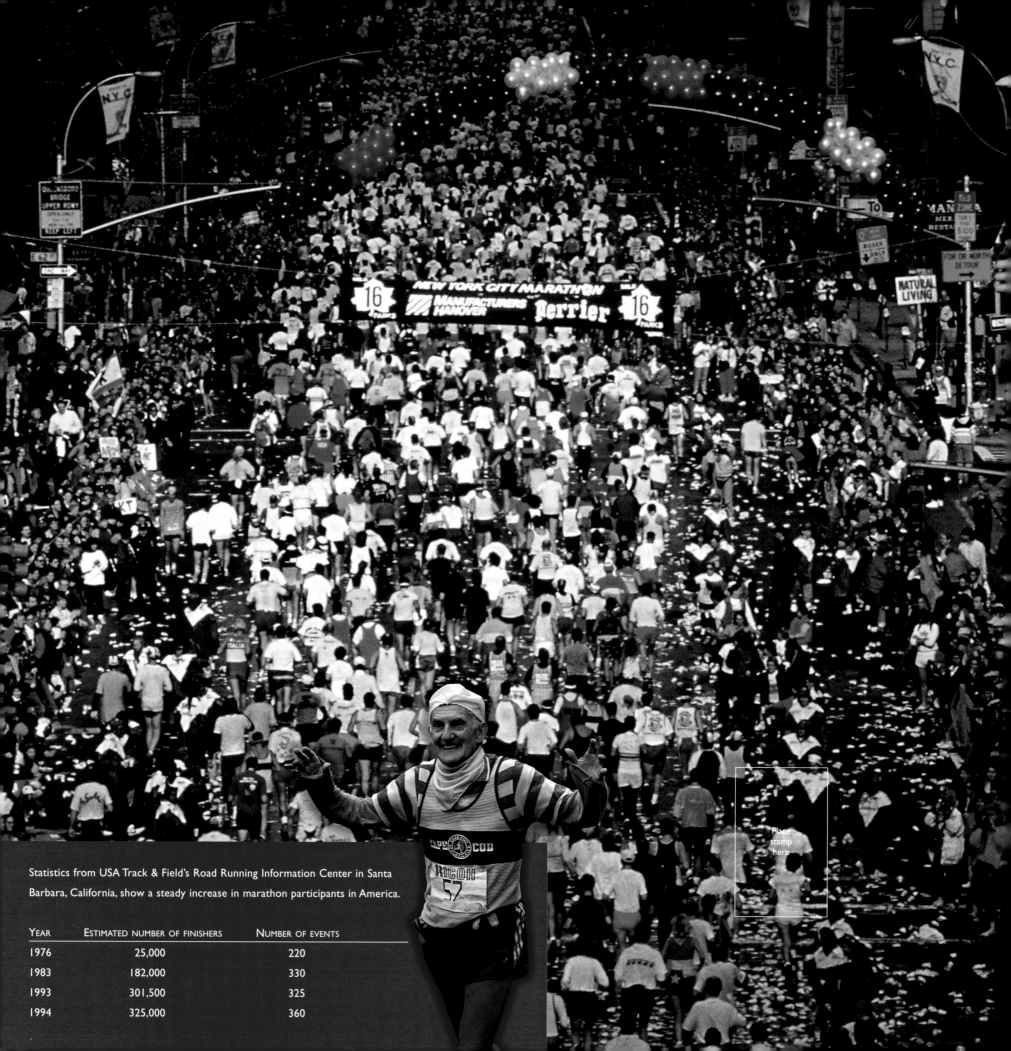

Statistics from USA Track & Field's Road Running Information Center in Santa Barbara, California, show a steady increase in marathon participants in America.

YEAR	ESTIMATED NUMBER OF FINISHERS	NUMBER OF EVENTS
1976	25,000	220
1983	182,000	330
1993	301,500	325
1994	325,000	360

MARATHON

O n a flat road runs the well-train'd runner,
He is lean and sinewy with muscular legs,
He is thinly clothed, he leans forward as he runs,
With lightly closed fists and arms partially rais'd.
—WALT WHITMAN, "BY THE ROADSIDE 1854," FROM *LEAVES OF GRASS*

The marathon is named for a legendary run made by Pheidippides, a Greek military messenger. In 490 B.C. Pheidippides hurried from Marathon to Athens, a distance of roughly the same length as today's marathon race, carrying news of a battle with the Persian army. Unfortunately, details of the message he carried have been lost in the mists of history; while one version of the story has Pheidippides carrying news of a Greek victory, another has him passing through on his way to seek help from Sparta.

The marathon is a supreme test of a runner's physiological and psychological limits. The first marathon held in the United States, in October 1896, began in Stamford, Connecticut, and finished at Columbus Circle in Manhattan. The marathon was modeled after a race run at the newly revived Olympic Games, held earlier that year in Athens.

In April 1897, the first Boston Marathon took place. There were 15 contestants. Since then, cities across the United States have staged their own marathons, including Chicago, Atlanta, San Francisco, Pittsburgh, Los Angeles, and Honolulu, with thousands of runners and millions of spectators. However, the Boston Marathon remains the world's oldest continually held annual marathon.

Recent decades have seen an increased interest in marathons and running in general, especially among women. The running boom, as it has been called, has encouraged more and more people to enter marathons, and the trend is not likely to reverse anytime soon.

This page (clockwise from top middle): shoes worn by Veikko Karvonen when he won the 1954 Boston Marathon; 18th-century re-creation of an ancient Greek map; Juma Ikangaa of Kenya in the 1992 Boston Marathon; Bill Rodgers' medal from the Boston Athletic Association for winning the 1975 marathon; runner getting water as she passes an aid station; 1925 Boston Marathon. Opposite page: New York City Marathon, 1989. Inset: John A. Kelley, age 80, running in the 1988 Boston Marathon.

Place
stamps
here

The 1936 Olympic Games were held in Berlin, in Hitler's
Germany. Hitler's bigoted views were well known, but they were not
shared by all Germans. Luz Long, a tall, blue-eyed, blond German athlete, advised Jesse
Owens, an African-American, during Owens' struggle to qualify in the long jump. Long,
the silver medalist, became the first person to congratulate Owens after his gold medal
jump—in full view of Hitler. Long and Owens became friends, and though Long was later
killed in World War II, Owens continued to correspond with his family.

OLYMPIC CLASSIC COLLECTION

MAY 2, WASHINGTON, D.C.

R ecords are ephemeral. The winning of an Olympic title is eternal.
—ROGER BANNISTER, WHO BROKE THE FOUR-MINUTE MILE
BARRIER IN 1954, BUT NEVER WON AN OLYMPIC MEDAL

In ancient Greece, a race was run in honor of Zeus every four years at Olympia. The winner was crowned with an olive wreath cut with a golden knife. Other games were eventually added to this quadrennial event, which became known as the Olympic Games, including a footrace run by heavily armed men and a four-horse chariot race. Perhaps the strangest "sport" was the pancration, a no-holds-barred contest between two men who fought until one gave up. Gouged eyes and broken bones were routine.

The Olympic Games were banned in the fourth century by Emperor Theodosius I, who banned all non-Christian rituals. Over 1,500 years later, the Games were revived by a Frenchman, Pierre de Coubertin. De Coubertin was greatly interested in sports; he led the movement to establish the Olympic Games in the modern age, and advocated wealthy patronage of working-class athletes.

The first Modern Olympic Games were held in 1896, in Athens, as a symbolic nod to their Greek origin. The highlight of the 1896 Games came when Spiridon Louis, a Greek shepherd, won the marathon. In gratitude for his victory, other Greeks offered him riches, but he accepted only a new cart and horse, which he needed to transport water to his village.

All wars were suspended during the ancient Olympic Games. The Modern Games, however, have been canceled three times due to conflicts: 1916, when they were disrupted by World War I; 1940, due to the Soviet invasion of Finland; and 1944, because of World War II. The Olympic Games have evolved into a welcome business boon for host cities and countries, easily generating over a billion dollars in revenue. Atlanta, Georgia, won the bid to host the 1996 Centennial Games, partly through the use of a virtual reality program allowing Olympic Committee members to visit Atlanta without leaving home.

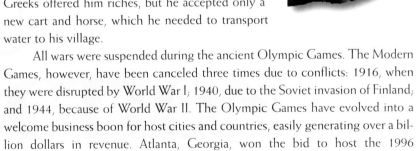

This page (clockwise from top): swimmer; gymnast; ancient Greek relief; javelin thrower; track athlete crossing finish line. Opposite page: ancient Greek vase painting of boxers. Inset: Jesse Owens at the 1936 Olympic Games, Berlin.

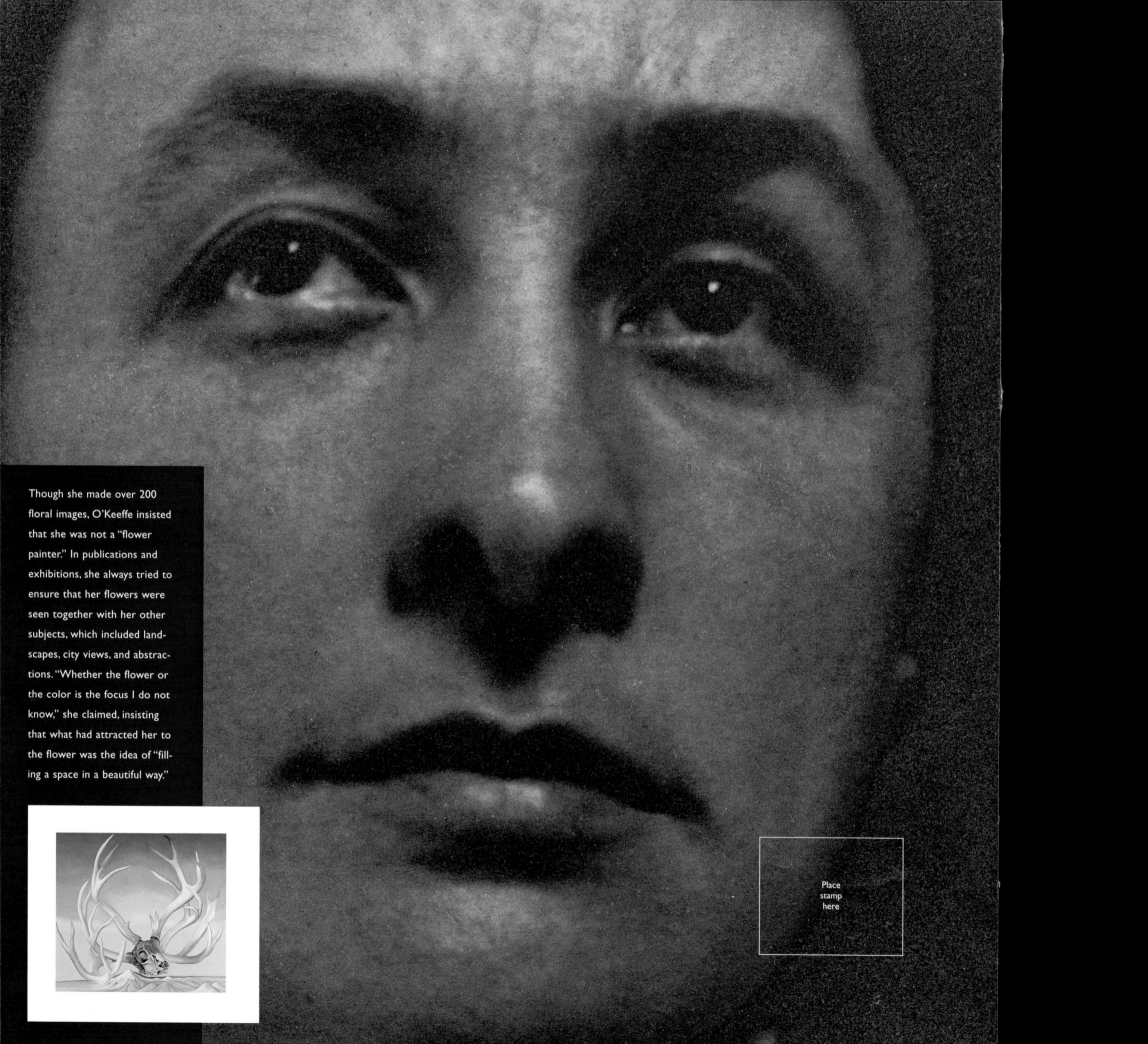

Though she made over 200 floral images, O'Keeffe insisted that she was not a "flower painter." In publications and exhibitions, she always tried to ensure that her flowers were seen together with her other subjects, which included landscapes, city views, and abstractions. "Whether the flower or the color is the focus I do not know," she claimed, insisting that what had attracted her to the flower was the idea of "filling a space in a beautiful way."

Place
stamp
here

Georgia O'Keeffe

MAY 23, SANTA FE, NEW MEXICO

O*ften, I've had the feeling that I could have been a much better painter and had far less recognition. It's just that what I do seems to move people today, in a way that I don't understand at all.*

—GEORGIA O'KEEFFE, AGE 86

Born in 1887, Georgia O'Keeffe became one of the foremost American painters of the 20th century. She spent her childhood on a farm in Wisconsin; her earliest memory was of the play of light on a quilt. An intelligent child, she could read music, but she later said she couldn't remember being taught how to read it. She told a girlhood friend she was going to be an artist. "I have no idea where that came from," she said later. "I just remember saying it."

As a young woman, O'Keeffe supported herself by working as a commercial artist, drawing lace and embroidery for advertisements, and then by teaching art. "I got so interested in teaching I wondered why I should be paid for it," she remembered later. In 1916, some of her drawings were exhibited by photographer Alfred Stieglitz at his "291 gallery" in New York City, without her prior permission or knowledge. When she confronted Stieglitz and demanded that he take her work down, he convinced her to change her mind. He continued to exhibit her work, and they were married in 1924.

O'Keeffe's flower paintings, first shown in 1925, ensured her celebrity. They were noted for their monumental scale, intense color, and sensuality. Ranging in size from the six-by-seven-foot *Miracle Flower* to tiny oils under one foot square, her flowers all appear monumental because they are set in space without perspective. She also gained notoriety by posing for a series of portraits taken by Stieglitz, some startlingly sensual.

After Stieglitz's death in 1946, O'Keeffe made her home in the New Mexico desert, about 70 miles northwest of Santa Fe, and concentrated on other pictorial subjects, including eroded hills and animal skulls. "A red hill doesn't touch everyone's heart as it touches mine," she wrote. O'Keeffe's paintings range from the abstract to the representational, with nature as her usual source of inspiration. She found the New Mexico landscape an inexhaustible resource. "Out here, half your work is done for you," she said.

O'Keeffe's fame became something of a burden to her in later life, when she fiercely guarded her privacy and solitude. She died in 1986.

This page (clockwise from top): view from O'Keeffe's studio at Abiquiu, New Mexico, 1960; paintbrushes; O'Keeffe in her studio at Abiquiu, circa 1953. Opposite page: O'Keeffe as a young woman, circa 1920. Inset: From the Faraway Nearby, a 1937 O'Keeffe oil.

Toward the end of the 19th century,
Tennessee women collaborated in
an effort to gain the right to vote.
In 1920, their commitment paid off
when their state's approval of the
Nineteenth Amendment won the
vote for all American women.

Tennessee Statehood

A

Agriculture and Commerce
— TENNESSEE STATE MOTTO

Tennessee takes its name from the Cherokee village of Tanasi, the capital of the Cherokee Nation from 1721 to 1730. Although the Cherokees were the largest group of original inhabitants in the state, Chickasaw, Choctaw, and Shawnee Indians also lived within its current borders.

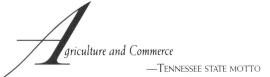

The first non-native settlers of Tennessee were mostly English, Scottish, and Irish. The German, Dutch, Swiss, and African populations were also sizable. In 1796, the region became the 16th state to join the Union, although its remote location, far from the federal American government, helped foster a spirit of independence for which the state is still recognized.

Tennessee earned its nickname, "The Volunteer State," in honor of the large number of Tennesseeans who served as volunteer soldiers with General Andrew Jackson during the War of 1812.

Today, Tennessee is a state so diverse in its geographic and cultural aspects that it resembles a miniature America. Land varies from the Great Smoky Mountains in the east to the flat Mississippi floodplain in the west. Tennessee has been recognized as an important site in the history of American music. The Grand Ole Opry in Nashville is a popular tourist attraction, as is Elvis Presley's mansion, Graceland, located in Memphis. W. C. Handy, the "Father of the Blues," Bessie Smith, the "Empress of the Blues," and Bill Monroe, the "Father of Bluegrass," all called Tennessee home. Several important literary figures have been associated with the state; of these, Mary Murfree (the pen name of Charles Egbert Craddock), Alex Haley, and Peter Taylor are among the most prominent.

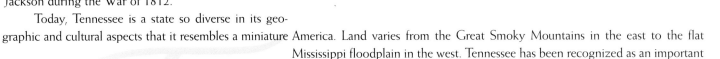

This page (clockwise from top): statue of composer W. C. Handy; "Blues" sign outside a Beale Street club in Memphis; rural Tennessee scene; 1982 World's Fair Sunsphere, Knoxville; Tootsies, a Nashville club; the iris, Tennessee's state flower. Opposite page: view in Great Smoky Mountains National Park. Inset: Tennessee suffragists.

29

The term "powwow" is given to a cultural gathering of American Indian people where traditional singing, dancing, and other group functions such as memorials and naming ceremonies take place. The word "powwow" is thought to come from an Algonquian word that is related to medicine or curing, *pauau* or *pau wau*.

Place
stamps
here

american indian dances

June 7, Oklahoma City, Oklahoma

W hen we dance, we enter a totally Indian world, and we shake the earth and touch the sky as we continue our culture.

—George Horse Capture, Àani (Gros Ventre tribe) Traditional dancer

Nothing symbolizes the richness and vitality of American Indian culture as much as its dances. Dancers perform at powwows, at social functions, in special ceremonies, and on theater stages.

One of the most electric performances is given by the Fancy dancer, usually a young man. Augmenting his regalia's stately black-and-white eagle feathers with brilliantly colored chicken feathers and elements such as ribbon and foil, this dancer does countless twists, acrobatics, and splits.

The Butterfly Dance is regularly performed in southwestern Pueblo Indian villages, where the butterfly is a symbol of peace, fertility, femininity, and agricultural abundance. In some villages, the dance is performed only after a formal request from the women, though Butterfly dancers usually appear in male/female pairs.

One of the oldest powwow dances performed in the Plains area is the Traditional Dance, said to have evolved out of an Omaha Indian tradition. Dancers wear the feathers of the golden eagle, a sacred and respected bird who delivers messages from the people below to The One Above.

Only experts can perform the difficult Hoop Dance, which involves creating designs with the hoops that represent elements of nature such as birds, turtles, and the earth. While keeping time with the music, the dancers move the hoops into a succession of changing patterns. It is widely believed that the hoop symbolizes the world or the universe.

In the cosmology and myth of the Tlingit people of southeastern Alaska, the Raven is a playful "trickster" figure, full of intelligence and curiosity. Credited with human and superhuman qualities, the Raven can transform itself into a person or any of various other manifestations. There are many dances featuring the Raven, which is portrayed by a masked dancer who makes appropriate calling sounds while flapping his or her "wings."

This page (clockwise from top middle): Traditional dancer; dancer at an inter-tribal festival, Bismarck, North Dakota, 1995; Raven dancer; dance event at Taos Pueblo, New Mexico; patterned American Indian beadwork. Opposite page: Fancy dancer's bustle. Inset: a rattle held by a Zuni dancer.

31

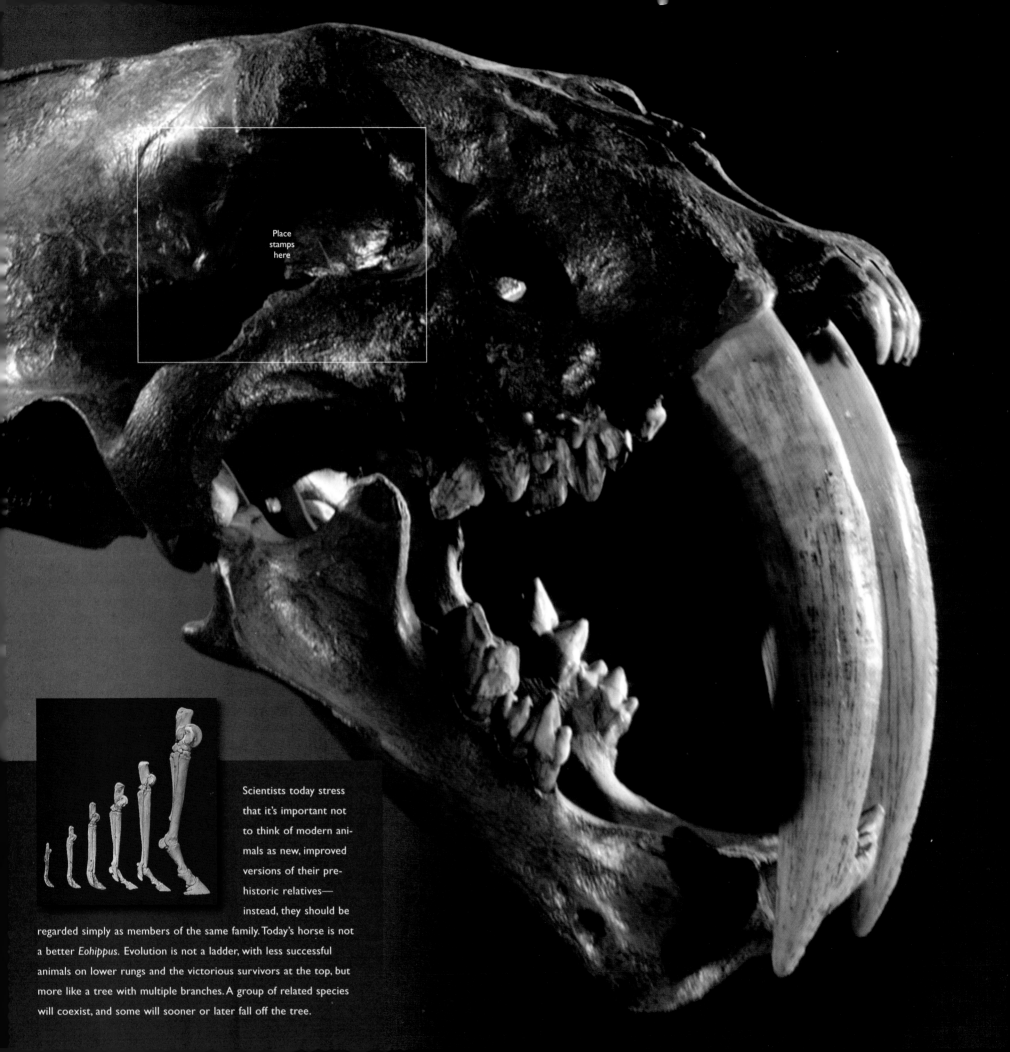

Place
stamps
here

Scientists today stress that it's important not to think of modern animals as new, improved versions of their prehistoric relatives—instead, they should be regarded simply as members of the same family. Today's horse is not a better *Eohippus*. Evolution is not a ladder, with less successful animals on lower rungs and the victorious survivors at the top, but more like a tree with multiple branches. A group of related species will coexist, and some will sooner or later fall off the tree.

Prehistoric Animals

T

he mystery of the beginning of all things is insoluble....
—Charles Darwin

Today's elephants, horses, and lions had some surprising relatives, revealed to us through fossils. The earliest known relative of the horse is called *Eohippus,* from the Greek words for "dawn" and "horse"—or dawn horse. Two prehistoric relatives of the elephant were the woolly mammoth and the mastodon. The saber-tooth cat sported fearsome fangs used for ripping into the flesh of its prey.

As big as today's lion, saber-tooth cats ranged across the Western Hemisphere until modern climates were established about 10,000 years ago. Their fangs were actually rather delicate, so it seems probable that the cats used them to attack the soft bellies of their prey, rather than risk breaking them on harder parts.

Mastodons, confined to North America, were tusked herbivores around ten feet tall. At the end of the last Ice Age, the forests they preferred began to make way for grassland. With the disappearance of their favored environment, mastodons lost not only sources of food but also their protective forest camouflage, making them easier targets for predators.

Unlike today's elephant, the woolly mammoth had small ears, which reduced the loss of body heat in frigid climates. Eyewitness accounts of the mammoth are preserved in the cave paintings of southern France. The first mammoth carcass found by modern human beings was discovered in 1799, embedded in the frozen bank of Siberia's Lena River.

Horses have evolved in America for millions of years. The earliest known horse, *Eohippus,* was about a foot tall and weighed only 20 pounds. It ranged across North America and Europe. Horses disappeared from North America at about the same time that man first entered the New World, but they made a triumphant reentry with the conquistadors.

This page (clockwise from top): cave painting of a horse in Lascaux, France; Eohippus; mastodon; scene with a saber-tooth cat; composite skeleton of a woolly mammoth. Opposite page: skull of saber-tooth cat. Inset: evolution of the horse's hind leg.

33

Place
stamp
here

The pink ribbon indicates support for the breast cancer awareness movement. As more and more women were diagnosed with breast cancer during the 1970s and 1980s, the amount of money spent on breast cancer research had not kept pace. Millions of women joined forces behind a common desire to end this disease. Their advocacy was responsible for a five-fold increase in funding for breast cancer research during the first half of the 1990s.

Breast Cancer Awareness

JUNE 15, WASHINGTON, D.C.

A ll of us continue to fight for more and better research to find the causes, prevention strategies, and cures for breast cancer. Without research, there is no end to this terrible waste of womanhood.

—MARY JO ELLIS KAHN, WOMAN LIVING WITH BREAST CANCER

Statistics suggest that one out of eight women in the United States will develop breast cancer sometime in her life. Although there is no known way to prevent it, if breast cancer is detected and treated early, a woman's chances of survival are very high.

A woman's risk for breast cancer increases with age; 80 percent of all breast cancers occur in women over 50 years old. A regular program of exams and mammography, however, may detect cancerous lumps early enough for successful treatment.

In many cases, breast cancer is first suspected when a small lump is detected. For this reason, many experts recommend monthly self-examination, routine breast exams by a physician, and regular mammograms, at different intervals according to a woman's age.

Breast cancer often can be detected before a lump can be felt. A mammogram—an x-ray of the breast—can identify many breast lumps up to two years before they can be detected by hand. Unfortunately, 10 to 15 percent of cancers may not be detected by mammograms. That's another good reason for regular clinical breast exams by physicians.

Finding a lump should not cause automatic alarm; the vast majority of breast lumps are benign. Monthly self-exams help a woman learn what is normal for her own breasts, so she will be more likely to notice if a change occurs. When a lump is found, a woman should consult her physician to determine the best course of action. If it is cancerous, four major kinds of treatment are available, alone or in combination: surgery, radiation, chemotherapy, and hormonal therapy. A number of new breast cancer treatments are being studied, including new anti-cancer drugs and genetic therapies.

Breast cancer is the most common form of cancer in women. Health educators try to disseminate information about breast cancer through every possible channel, from the Internet to placards on city buses. October has been designated National Breast Cancer Awareness Month, designed to raise public awareness of the disease and promote early detection.

BREAST CANCER

For the next Generation:

Michelle Kahn, Daughter
Barbara Kahn, Daughter
Amy Tate, Niece

FIND NEW WAYS

FIGHTING FOR OUR LIVES

TAKING CHARGE
1. KNOW YOUR OPTIONS
2. SPEAK UP
3. TAKE RESPONSIBILITY
4. ASK QUESTIONS
5. TALK TO OTHERS
6. 2ND + 3RD OPINIONS
7. DON'T PANIC

This page (clockwise from top): nurse and patient at mammogram machine; breast cancer awareness marchers; breast cancer support group; breast cancer poster. Opposite page: breast cancer patient with her mother and daughter. Inset: the pink ribbon, emblem of the breast cancer awareness movement.

35

In May 1955, night scenes for *Rebel Without a Cause* were shot at Griffith Park Planetarium in Los Angeles. The lights set up for filming prompted a rash of concerned telephone calls from members of the surrounding community, who thought that a forest fire had broken out. As a lasting tribute to Dean, a statue of him was erected in the park in 1988. Today, his fans often go there to pay their respects.

Place stamp here

James Dean

June 24, Burbank, California

I *f a man can bridge the gap between life and death…if he can live on after he's died, then maybe he was a great man.*

—James Dean

James Byron Dean was born in 1931 in Marion, Indiana. At the age of four, he moved with his parents to California, where his mother died five years later. Young Jimmy accompanied her body on the train from Los Angeles back to Indiana, where he was raised on the farm of an aunt and uncle near Fairmount.

His participation in high school drama productions inspired Dean to become an actor. In one of these productions, a Halloween spoof called *Goon With the Wind*, he played Frankenstein's monster.

In June of 1949, he took a bus to California to join his father and begin college coursework. He attended classes at Santa Monica City College and at UCLA but withdrew after a year to concentrate on his career. He had already finished his first professional acting job, earning $30 for appearing in a television commercial as one of several teenagers dancing around a jukebox while singing about Pepsi-Cola.

A clue to the galvanizing effect that James Dean's later performances would have on audiences came when he appeared as John the Apostle in a television drama aired on Easter Sunday 1951. In response to his performance, girls at a parochial school formed the Immaculate Heart James Dean Appreciation Society.

On the advice of his acting coach, James Whitmore, Dean went to New York in September 1951 to look for work in the theater. In October of the following year he landed his first leading role, in a play that ran less than a week. Steady television work came his way throughout this period. In his free time Dean fostered his other talents, taking dance classes with Eartha Kitt and studying photography with Roy Schatt. In April 1954, director Elia Kazan signed him for *East of Eden*. Critics and audiences alike were mesmerized by Dean's performance as the misunderstood Cal Trask, and he was quickly cast in two additional films, *Rebel Without a Cause* and *Giant*, both released after his death. Dean was killed in an automobile accident in September 1955.

In each of his three major film roles, Dean played a lonely, misunderstood outsider. He helped to define a new style of American film acting, with a heightened physical dimension suggesting feelings that couldn't be put into words. His stature in the history of cinema is monumental.

This page (clockwise from top): Dean's last visit to the farm where he was raised near Fairmount, Indiana; a French poster for Giant; *Dean in Fairmont, Indiana, in 1955, reading from the complete works of the poet, James Whitcomb Riley; with Julie Harris in* East of Eden. *Opposite page: James Dean, photographed by Phil Stern* © James Dean® James Dean Foundation Trust C/o CMG Worldwide, Indpl., IN. Inset: Dean in 1955

Place
stamps
here

Young America invented its own mythology;
Paul Bunyan, Pecos Bill, John Henry, and mighty
Casey are four of its most compelling heroes. Their stories have a kind of poetic
truth, essential to any understanding of the American character. Oscar Wilde
summed it up in the following relevant comment: "Where there is no exaggeration
there is no love," he wrote, "and where there is no love there is no understanding."

Folk Heroes

I f American folklore is, on the whole, closer to history than to mythology, it is because America as a whole is closer to the beginnings of settlement and to the oral and written sources of local history.

—BENJAMIN BOTKIN, AMERICAN FOLKLORIST

When the United States emerged victorious from World War I, it was clear that it had become a world power. Triumph abroad and burgeoning development at home sparked the nation's appetite for heroes; this hunger seemed insatiable, and people turned to folklore to supply the need. Folk heroes were America's earliest supermen.

Paul Bunyan and Pecos Bill casually triumphed over hardships associated with American extremes of behavior and weather, reminding people of what had been accomplished and endured in building their new world. Paul Bunyan is a larger-than-life representation of the loggers who chopped down acres and acres of American trees. Stories about him were possibly being told as early as 1850, though he didn't appear in print until the 20th century.

Pecos Bill, the cowboy whose feats included digging the Rio Grande, embodied the wildness of America's Western frontier. His fame spread to cowboys in Argentina and Australia.

He first appeared in print in 1920, when author Edward O'Reilly combined cowboy folklore with the comic tone of tall tales. Many other writers embraced O'Reilly's creation in plays, books, articles, and poems.

Although the history is clouded, John Henry probably lived and worked as a "steel driver," drilling holes into rock for explosives to blast railroad tunnels through mountains. Black workers soon began to sing about John Henry's legendary race with the newly developed steam drill. In these widespread songs and tales, he is the heroic working man fighting for his job as machines take over. He serves as a symbol of the contributions black Americans have made in industrializing America.

The mighty Casey, whose disappointing turn at bat made him immortal, was created in 1888 in the famous comic verse by Ernest Lawrence Thayer and has no basis in historical fact. Written during an era of baseball fever, it was immortalized by performer William DeWolf Hopper, who claimed to have recited it over 10,000 times. To many, Casey's story is really a backhanded compliment to the athletes who play America's favorite sport. Even though they sometimes disappoint us, we still love them.

This page (clockwise from top): railroad workers laboring on the Great Bend Tunnel, circa 1880; Texas cowboys; statue, Casey at the Bat. Opposite page (clockwise from top right): Pecos Bill; mighty Casey; Paul Bunyan; John Henry. Inset: 19th-century American centennial flag.

Place
stamp
here

A young American, Robert
Garrett, won first place in the
discus throw at the 1896
Olympic Games. As a student at
Princeton University, Garrett saw
a drawing of an ancient discus, had a replica made, and practiced with
it. The copy was too heavy, and he lost interest until he was at the
Games in Athens and realized that the modern discus was much
lighter. On a whim, he entered the event and won it on his final throw.

OLYMPIC ANNIVERSARY SHEET

JULY 19, ATLANTA, GEORGIA

I've always viewed it as recreation. I don't need a pot of gold to make me train hard.
— AL OERTER, FOUR-TIME OLYMPIC GOLD MEDALIST

The discus throw was part of the pentathlon, a series of five track and field contests, in the ancient Greek Olympic Games. In the Modern Olympic Games, first held in 1896 in Athens, the discus throw is held as a separate event. A modern discus weighs just over four and a half pounds, about ten pounds lighter than those used by the ancient Greeks, but the technique used in throwing both has changed little over the centuries.

The most successful discus thrower to date is Al Oerter, an American who won the gold medal four times. Oerter has been referred to as the last of a breed of gentlemen athletes who competed for the sheer joy of play. To questions regarding his technique, he replies, "It's all in the mind."

Each time Al Oerter won a gold medal in the discus throw, he bettered his previous performance. He was the first American track and field performer to win four gold medals in the same event in consecutive Olympic Games. In the 1956 Games, held in Melbourne, Australia, Oerter's throw was 184 feet, 11 inches. By the time he won his fourth gold medal, in Mexico City in 1968, the length of his throw had increased almost 28 feet.

One of the most elegant representations of the sport is Myron's magnificent bronze *Discobolus*, or *Discus Thrower*, created about 450 B.C. This life-size sculpture shows Myron's mastery of human movement by representing the athlete bending forward at the moment of highest tension, paused between the backswing and the release of the discus. Cicero wrote, "Myron's works are not yet close enough to truth and yet one cannot hesitate to call them beautiful."

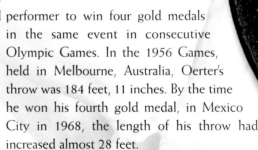

This page (clockwise from top): 1920 Olympic poster, Antwerp, Belgium; an ancient metal discus; Greek vase showing discus thrower with trainer; woman throwing discus. Background: Myron's Discus Thrower. Opposite page: athlete competing in discus throw event. Inset: Robert Garrett.

The story of Marx Goettsch typifies the experience of immigrants to Iowa in the 19th century. Trained as a shoemaker, Goettsch arrived in Davenport at the age of 24, with his wife and one child. A successful businessman, he bought five lots in Davenport and built a house on each one, becoming a prosperous landlord. Goettsch and his wife had five sons: Two earned Ph.D.s, two more became medical doctors, and the fifth became an engineer. All seven grandchildren, including two boys and five girls, became professionals. For the Goettsch family, as for so many others, Iowa was truly a land of opportunity.

Place stamp here

IOWA STATEHOOD

AUGUST 1, DUBUQUE, IOWA

*O*ur Liberties We Prize, and Our Rights We Will Maintain

—IOWA STATE MOTTO

The first Europeans known to have set foot in Iowa were two French explorers, Louis Joliet and Father Jacques Marquette. In 1673, they stepped on shore near the junction of the Iowa and Mississippi Rivers. Nearly 20 different American Indian tribes had preceded them; the largest of these were the Sioux, Sauk, and Meskwaki. The Meskwaki still make their home in Iowa.

Non-native settlement didn't begin in earnest until 1833, when the first major influx of pioneers arrived. As settlers pushed into the state's interior, they encountered endless miles of prairie. The land was vast and cheap, but it did pose some problems. Prairie fires swept through thousands of acres, sometimes annually. Timber, normally used for everything from building material to fuel, was scarce.

The settlers were forced to adapt to their new environment, but they were rewarded by abundant harvests from Iowa's rich and fertile land.

In 1846, Iowa became the 29th state to enter the Union. More settlers came in the 1850s, tripling the population of the state. Frontier towns, with permanent churches and schools, were established throughout the rest of the century. Railroad companies began constructing a network of lines to connect Iowa's farmers with markets across the country. The railroads also fostered the growth of farm-related manufacturing, which became one of the leading industries in the state.

Today, Iowa's economy is still firmly based on the land that attracted the early settlers. Agriculture and related manufacturing are still principal businesses of the state, with tourism also contributing a significant portion of revenue. Educational institutions are a major employer for the population. There are three state universities in Iowa and several private colleges.

This page (clockwise from top): State Capitol, Des Moines; blue-ribbon corn on display at Iowa State Fair; the American goldfinch, Iowa's state bird; an Iowa farm scene; a modern-day re-creation of early farming techniques at Living History Farm. Opposite page: This round barn in Allamakee County, dates from the early 20th century. Inset: Davenport, Iowa, circa 1910.

Place stamp here

E.T. KASH
DRINK
Dr. Pepper
GOOD FOR LIFE!

PURE

E.T. KASH
GENERAL STORE

E.T. KASH
AL STORE

U.S. POST OFFICE Landsaw KY.

In the early days of the Rural Free Delivery system, many rural mail routes were nicknamed "No Man's Land"—made up of unpaved country roads, some nearly impassable in bad weather. Many rural routes still include dirt roads today. Asked how many holes there were in the roads of his route, a rural carrier once replied, "Just one. It begins when I leave town, and ends when I reach the brick street returning, except for three miles of gravel road."

Rural Free Delivery

AUGUST 7, CHARLESTON, WEST VIRGINIA

*I*t would be difficult to point to any like expenditure of public money which has been more generously appreciated by the people....
—POSTMASTER GENERAL JAMES A. GARY, ANNUAL REPORT OF OCTOBER 1897

Before rural mail carriers began operating their mobile post offices, farmers had to travel into the nearest town for news of the world. The first five official rural delivery routes, operating out of Jefferson County, West Virginia, were established in 1896. Within three years, routes existed in 40 states and one territory; today, more than 55,000 routes serve over 25 million customers in every state of the union.

In a sense, the concept of the Rural Free Delivery system was first developed in 1868 in Norwood, Georgia, when a former slave named Jerry Elliot was hired to carry mail for six families. Each morning Elliot walked into Norwood from his cabin on the land of one of these families. While in town, he picked up the mail from the postmaster, and he subsequently made deliveries over his route. Along the way, Elliot gathered outgoing mail from his customers, carrying it to town in the afternoon. Georgia Congressman Tom Watson, then a young store clerk in Norwood, remembered this arrangement in 1893 and drafted legislation for the permanent establishment of a nationwide free rural delivery system. The idea was approved by Congress but rejected by the new Postmaster General, William S. Bissell.

Previously, in 1891, free rural mail delivery had been made available on a limited, "experimental" basis. Farmers and other constituents across America had petitioned Congress to establish such a system nationwide, arguing that they were entitled to the same government services as those provided for their city-dwelling cousins, who had enjoyed free mail delivery since 1863. They pointed out that it would be more efficient and economical for one person to deliver the mail to several households than to have someone from each house travel to town individually.

Traditionally, rural carriers have been a vital link between their community and the outside world. Their reliable and friendly service is legendary. Today, the National Rural Letter Carriers' Association represents over 92,000 members; 23 percent of all carrier deliveries are made by rural carriers. The longest regular route is 179.75 miles per day, and the shortest is 3.05 miles per day.

This page (clockwise from top): a farmer receives mail, 1939; an early rural mail carrier; a four cents stamp issued in 1913; a woman receives mail on a rural route in York County, Maine. Opposite page: a rural carrier leaves the Landsaw, Kentucky, post office, 1940. Inset: a Texas cowboy mailing a letter, 1909.

A story in the *Columbus Enquirer Sun* in 1880 reported that the captain of the *Rebecca Everingham* "is specially noted for his courtesies to the ladies...he is as kind and thoughtful of his female passengers as if the discovery of a partner was his sole object in life."

Place stamps here

RIVERBOATS

Your true pilot cares nothing about anything on earth but the river, and his pride in his occupation surpasses the pride of kings.

—Mark Twain, *Life on the Mississippi*

Before they were eclipsed by railroads and a closing frontier, thousands of steam-powered riverboats carried cargo and passengers throughout America.

The regal *Robt. E. Lee* became famous as the fastest boat on the Mississippi River when she outraced the *Natchez* from New Orleans to St. Louis in 1870. Her owner, Captain John W. Cannon, was described in the *Marine Journal* as "never happier than when exploiting the good qualities of the *LEE*." The *Robt. E. Lee* was dismantled in 1876.

The sternwheeler *Far West*, a ruggedly built mountain boat, carried cargo and passengers on the Upper Missouri River between Sioux City and Fort Benton, winning fame when she brought survivors of Custer's 1876 Little Bighorn expedition—members of Major Reno's troops—down the Yellowstone River. The *Far West* sank on a snag in 1883.

The *Rebecca Everingham* carried passengers, agricultural products, and finished goods between Florida and Georgia, along the Apalachicola and Chattahoochee Rivers. In 1884, a fire burned her to the waterline. The *Columbus* (Georgia) *Enquirer Sun* reported that it would be "some time before another boat will be…such a favorite with the traveling public."

Built in 1872 to carry commuters along the East River between Harlem and lower Manhattan, the *Sylvan Dell* was forced to find other employment when the Third Avenue elevated railway was completed in 1883. She carried New Yorkers on pleasure excursions until 1889, when she moved to the Delaware River, ferrying commuters between Philadelphia and Salem, New Jersey. She sank in Salem Creek in 1919.

The *Bailey Gatzert* was the type of steamboat favored on the West Coast, with a single smokestack, enclosed superstructure, and covered sternwheel. She provided transportation between Seattle, Tacoma, and Olympia, Washington. In 1918, the *Bailey Gatzert* was converted into an automobile ferry. She was taken out of service in 1923.

This page (clockwise from top): the U.S. Mail Packet Chesapeake; *promotional fan for People's Line Steamers; the* Far West; *riverboats at New Orleans. Opposite page: an ornate riverboat salon. Inset: the Rebecca Everingham.*

During the golden age of jazz, big bands were so popular that Hollywood producers chose to feature the orchestras in films. Glenn Miller and his band appeared in *Sun Valley Serenade* and *Orchestra Wives*. Benny Goodman and his band appeared in *The Big Broadcast of 1937*, *Hollywood Hotel*, and others. Tommy and Jimmy Dorsey appeared as themselves in *The Fabulous Dorseys*.

Place stamps here

BIG BAND LEADERS

SEPTEMBER 11, NEW YORK, NEW YORK

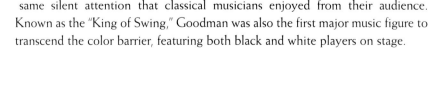

A *wonderful era, a time when the guy took the gal in his arms to dance with her....*
—LES BROWN, BANDLEADER

With swing, jazz, blues, and boogie-woogie, the big band leaders took American music to new heights of popularity.

Although he and his band were the embodiment of Kansas City jazz, **Count Basie** was born in Red Bank, New Jersey, and wound up in the Midwest by chance. Basie made his reputation with various bands in Kansas City. By the mid-1930s he had become a leader in his own right, recognized for his highly sensitive, blues-oriented style of short melodic phrases, leads, and cues. The Basie band's recordings, including "Jumpin' at the Woodside" and "One O'Clock Jump," are among the finest of the period and brought Basie international fame.

No band represents the sentimental and romantic yearnings of the War years better than **Glenn Miller**'s. Known for the sound of its characteristic clarinet lead doubling the tenor sax an octave higher, Miller's band achieved musical immortality with dance songs such as "In the Mood" and "Moonlight Serenade." As a patriotic gesture, Miller disbanded his group and joined the Armed Forces in 1942; two years later, his plane disappeared in bad weather over the English Channel.

Tutored in music from an early age by their father, **Tommy and Jimmy Dorsey** performed throughout their native Pennsylvania as tots. They were in great demand in the New York music scene of the late 1920s and 1930s. They formed their own orchestra in 1934, but frequent disagreements caused their breakup the following year. Jimmy stayed with the band, building it into a leading dance orchestra. Tommy organized a band of his own, which became known for its ballads. Jimmy played reeds, excelling on clarinet and saxophone; Tommy played trombone. They are remembered for such songs as Jimmy's "Oodles of Noodles" and Tommy's "Song of India."

Benny Goodman was a child prodigy, playing in vaudeville houses by the time he was 13 years old. One of the first true virtuosi to appear in the jazz world, Goodman had a technical ability that was matched by his capacity for swinging emotion. He was the first jazz artist to achieve the same silent attention that classical musicians enjoyed from their audience. Known as the "King of Swing," Goodman was also the first major music figure to transcend the color barrier, featuring both black and white players on stage.

This page (clockwise from top): Glenn Miller and orchestra members; Count Basie; record label from the Glenn Miller Orchestra's recording of the Gershwin song "I Got Rhythm;" Benny Goodman; Tommy (left) and Jimmy Dorsey. Opposite page: couples dancing at Steeplechase Park, June 1944. Inset: a scene at Harlem's Savoy Ballroom.

Photo of Glenn Miller is licensed by the heirs of Glenn Miller. Represented by CMG Worldwide, Inc., Indianapolis, Indiana.

Place
stamps
here

The songwriters honored on these stamps were among the first to take advantage of electrical recording technology and radio. Their work was heard by more people, more quickly, than had ever been possible before. Each of the four contributed familiar, classic, and enduring songs that became part of the American cultural fabric, even penetrating distant corners of the world. Today, popular music is all-pervasive, and probably heard at least once during the day by every person in America—in corridors, in elevators, in restaurants, over telephone lines, on television, in passing cars, or even on a pair of headphones worn by someone else.

SONGWRITERS

SEPTEMBER 11, NEW YORK, NEW YORK

T

he art of music above all other arts is the expression of the soul of a nation.
—RALPH VAUGHAN WILLIAMS, ENGLISH COMPOSER

This quartet of songwriters contributed an astounding number of standards to America's popular song repertoire.

Hoagy Carmichael was unusual among songwriters for having contributed many songs to both popular and jazz repertoires. As a boy, he studied piano with his mother, who played ragtime and popular songs in silent-movie theaters in Bloomington, Indiana. With his favorite lyricist, Johnny Mercer, Carmichael composed numerous hits, including "In the Cool, Cool, Cool of the Evening" and "Skylark." "Stardust," published in 1929, became one of the world's most frequently recorded standards.

The lyricist **Dorothy Fields** came from one of the foremost families of American musical theater. Her first successes were songs written for revues in collaboration with the composer Jimmy McHugh, including "On the Sunny Side of the Street." She also collaborated with Jerome Kern on the film versions of *Roberta* and *Swing Time*. Most of her writing was done for the Broadway stage and Hollywood movies. Fields' work was characterized by a colloquial turn of phrase and deceptively simple casualness.

Johnny Mercer's first successful song was "Lazybones," published in 1933, and subsequently he contributed lyrics to over 1,000 other popular songs. His lyrics cover a wide range of styles; his particular gift was for incorporating Southern vernacular speech and images of country settings into a more cultivated urban genre. This talent, reflecting his Savannah, Georgia, upbringing, is highlighted in such songs as "Blues in the Night" and "Moon River." Mercer also wrote both words and music to many songs.

Composer **Harold Arlen** was born in Buffalo, New York, where he played piano in local movie houses before moving to New York City. In 1929, he began a collaboration with lyricist Ted Koehler, producing several memorable songs for Harlem's famed Cotton Club, including "Between the Devil and the Deep Blue Sea" and "Stormy Weather." These songs drew on Arlen's love for jazz and blues. During a hiatus from the musical stage, Arlen composed songs for films, including "Over the Rainbow" for *The Wizard of Oz*.

This page (clockwise from top): Johnny Mercer, 1954; sheet music cover of Johnny Mercer and Matt Malneck tune; Hoagy Carmichael, 1945; Harold Arlen, 1934. Opposite page: Dorothy Fields. Inset: dancers in 1944.

51

Place
stamp
here

The first edition of *The Great Gatsby*, published in April 1925, sold for two dollars a copy. In a congratulatory letter to Fitzgerald, T. S. Eliot wrote, "In fact it seems to me to be the first step American fiction has taken since Henry James." One reviewer, Gilbert Seldes, remarked that Fitzgerald "has mastered his talents and gone soaring in a beautiful flight…. He has now something of extreme importance to say; and it is good fortune for us that he knows how to say it." *The Great Gatsby* continues to sell about 300,000 copies a year.

F. Scott Fitzgerald

SEPTEMBER 27, ST. PAUL, MINNESOTA

So we beat on, boats against the current, borne back ceaselessly into the past.
—F. SCOTT FITZGERALD, *THE GREAT GATSBY*

Born in St. Paul, Minnesota, in 1896, F. Scott Fitzgerald became one of America's greatest writers. His stories and novels, often incorporating autobiographical elements, tapped the pulse of the Jazz Age (a term he coined).

Fitzgerald's most popular book was *The Great Gatsby*, an undisputed classic published in 1925. In Fitzgerald's characteristically beautiful prose, this complexly constructed novel tells the story of James Gatz, a poor boy who changes his name to Jay Gatsby and makes a fortune, partly through bootlegging liquor. Gatsby's tragedy results from his unshakable hope that his money can erase the past and capture Daisy, the girl of his dreams, now married to millionaire Tom Buchanan. But Gatsby's unwavering devotion to the woman he loves and to the American dream of success—in short, to his ideals—are what make him great.

Fitzgerald's work is instilled with an understanding of the American class system. His maternal grandfather, an Irish immigrant, built himself into a prosperous businessman, while his father had breeding but no fortune. In

the younger Fitzgerald's sophomore year at Princeton University, he had a disappointing love affair with a girl from a wealthy family, in which the rejection he ultimately suffered was seen as the natural result of his social standing.

In 1920, Fitzgerald married Zelda Sayre, the beautiful daughter of a Montgomery, Alabama, judge. They spent money lavishly and moved restlessly from place to place, living in and around New York City and also in St. Paul. Known as inveterate party types, they also traveled in Europe and spent several years in France. His short stories could command princely sums from the magazines of the era—the *Saturday Evening Post* paid him fees as high as $4,000 per piece—but the Fitzgeralds spent more than they earned.

When America sank into the Great Depression, Fitzgerald's life and career followed a similar trajectory. Zelda suffered a mental breakdown in 1930; she moved in and out of sanatoriums for the rest of her life. Fitzgerald's own struggle with alcoholism nearly ruined him. He now sold stories for as little as $250 each. In debt, struggling to pay Zelda's hospital bills and to pay for his daughter's schooling, Fitzgerald went to Hollywood in 1937, where he wrote screenplays for a salary of $1,000 a week. He died of a heart attack in 1940, while writing *The Last Tycoon*. Since then, his work has enjoyed increasing acclaim.

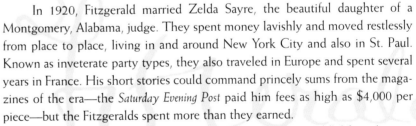

This page (clockwise from top): dancing the Charleston in the 1948 Paramount picture, The Great Gatsby; Fitzgerald's personalized briefcase; movie poster for The Last Tycoon, starring Robert De Niro; Fitzgerald and his daughter, Frances (called "Scottie"), in 1928. Opposite page: F. Scott Fitzgerald and his wife, Zelda. Inset: a first edition of The Great Gatsby brought $19,800 at auction in 1993.

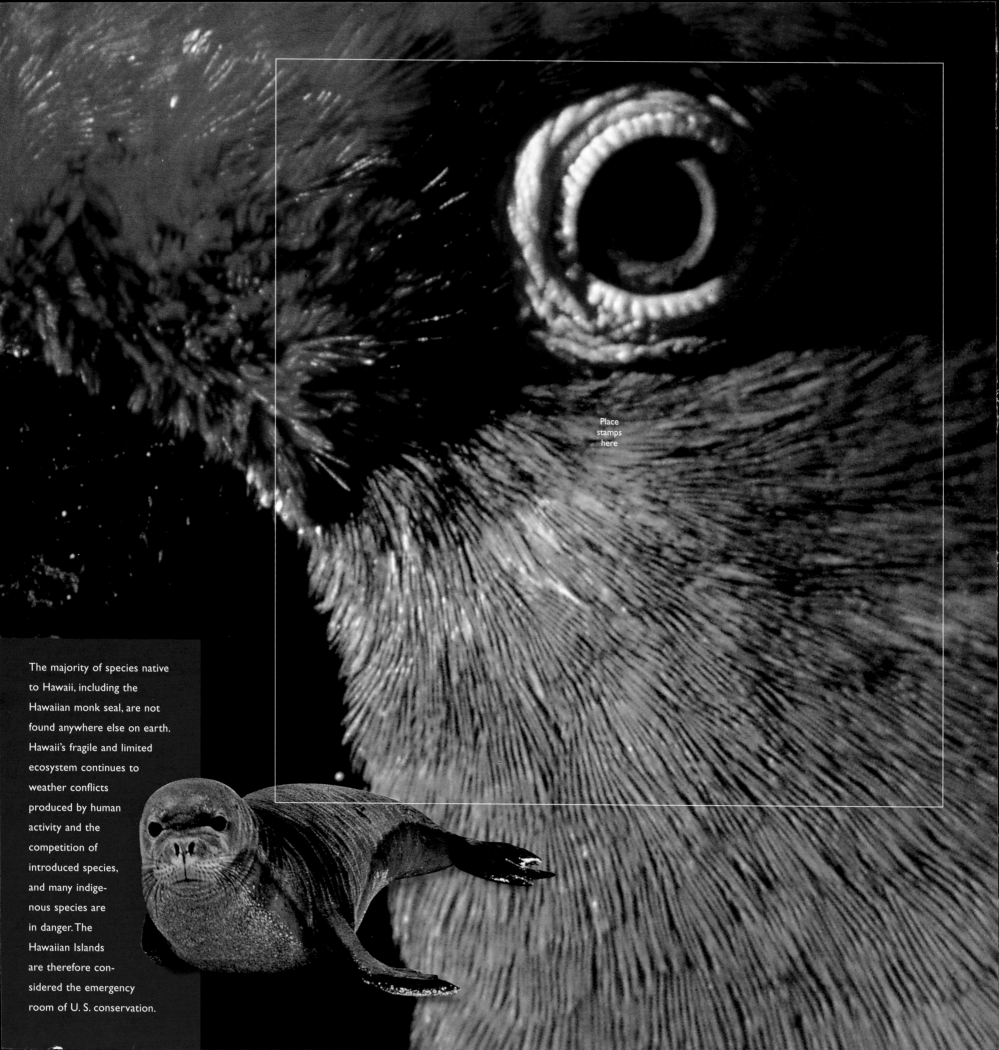

Place
stamps
here

The majority of species native
to Hawaii, including the
Hawaiian monk seal, are not
found anywhere else on earth.
Hawaii's fragile and limited
ecosystem continues to
weather conflicts
produced by human
activity and the
competition of
introduced species,
and many indige-
nous species are
in danger. The
Hawaiian Islands
are therefore con-
sidered the emergency
room of U. S. conservation.

Endangered Species

T*hese species of fish, wildlife, and plants are of esthetic, ecological, educational, historical, recreational, and scientific value to the Nation and its people....*
—FROM THE ENDANGERED SPECIES ACT OF 1973

The Endangered Species Act is one of the world's most widely known environmental laws. Under its authority, two federal agencies, the U. S. Fish and Wildlife Service and the National Marine Fisheries Service, review candidate species to determine whether they should be listed as threatened or endangered. Hundreds of plant and animal species have disappeared in the United States since the time of the Pilgrims. In 1973, when President Richard Nixon signed the Endangered Species Act into law, 109 species were listed. The total is now near 1,000.

Typically, endangered and threatened species face a variety of threats. These include loss of habitat, the presence of pesticides and other toxins in the environment, and competition or predation by introduced species.

Once a plant or animal species is added to the endangered and threatened list, ingenious techniques may be used to restore a population. For example, California condor chicks are bred in captivity and fed by scientists wearing hand puppets that look like condor parents, keeping human contact to a minimum.

Our growing understanding of the interrelationships among plants, animals, and humans dictates that we must assume that all of earth's life-forms are important, many for reasons yet unknown. Recently, the Pacific yew, formerly cut down on the assumption that it was worthless, was discovered to yield taxol, a cancer-fighting compound. A member of the salmon family, the coho, lives the first part of its life in fresh water and then, in preparation for adult life at sea, grows large amounts of new nerve fiber. The coho has become valuable to researchers seeking knowledge about brain and spinal injuries. Perhaps the most persuasive argument for the preservation of biodiversity is that plants and animals have already saved human lives and are likely to continue to do so in the future.

This page (clockwise from top middle): ocelot; black-footed ferret; Schaus swallowtail butterfly; American crocodile; San Francisco garter snake. Opposite page: thick-billed parrot. Inset: Hawaiian monk seal.

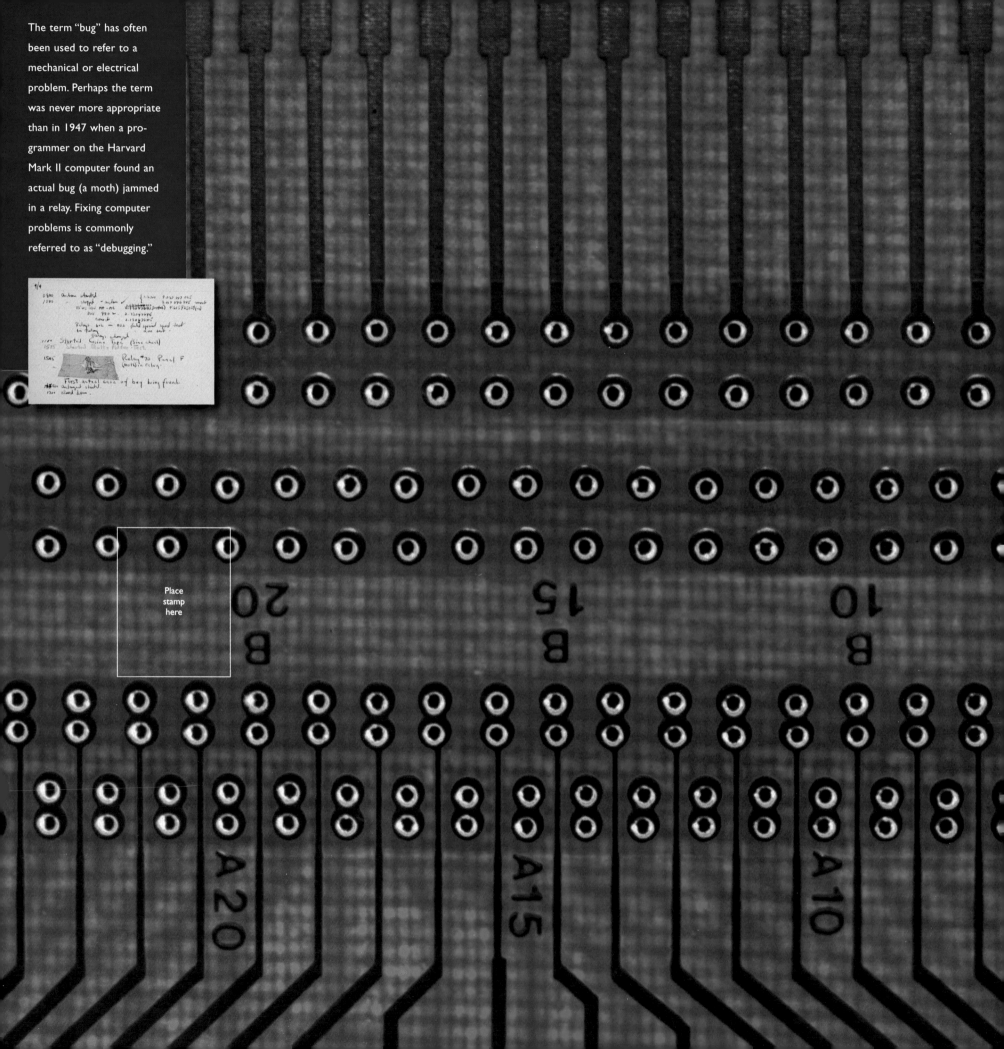

The term "bug" has often been used to refer to a mechanical or electrical problem. Perhaps the term was never more appropriate than in 1947 when a programmer on the Harvard Mark II computer found an actual bug (a moth) jammed in a relay. Fixing computer problems is commonly referred to as "debugging."

Place stamp here

COMPUTER TECHNOLOGY

Computing is not about computers anymore. It is about living.
—Nicholas Negroponte, *Being Digital*

The first programmable electronic digital computer was ENIAC, the Electronic Numerical Integrator and Computer, publicly unveiled in 1946 at the University of Pennsylvania. It consisted of 40 units, all wired together, and virtually filled a room the size of a gym. At the time, no one thought that this technology would explode into the industry it is today. Once exclusively used by government and big business, computers are moving into private hands more and more.

Digital computers today manipulate more than numbers; for example, music is digitally recorded on compact discs. Through the Internet, a worldwide network of computers, digital text can be transmitted almost instantly, without regard to traditional physical and geographic limits. E-mail conversations can cross continents and oceans quickly and economically.

There may be no more powerful educational tool than the interactive computer. Students of all ages and all levels learn practically everything on computers with spectacular ease. Airline pilots are currently trained on flight simulators to practice making the life-or-death decisions that may confront them later. Soon, it may be customary for medical school students in simulated operating theaters to duplicate the actual operations performed by their teachers.

With greater numbers of people logging on daily, the computer revolution will continue. Computers will make it easier for millions of people to get information and entertainment tailored to their individual interests—in essence, users will have the capability to read a personalized newspaper or watch personalized TV.

Someday, with the aid of computers, we may no longer forget where we put things, from our cars to our keys—or, more accurately, we'll still forget, but it won't matter; our things will tell us where they are. Our alarm clock might communicate with our coffee maker and electric lights and call for the weather report as well—it might even wake us a little early on snowy days.

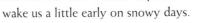

This page (clockwise from top): an experimental image created on a computer; John von Neumann and the AIS computer, circa 1952; child playing a computer game; adult playing a video game at the Cyberscope Store; 35-millimeter camera containing a computer chip. Opposite page: circuit board. Inset: a "bug" (moth) found jammed in a relay in 1947.

The most important commissions for artists of the Renaissance and baroque periods in Europe came from the Catholic Church, European courts, or wealthy aristocratic families. Paolo de Matteis, the artist whose work is featured on this year's traditional holiday stamp, worked for all three types of patrons—including the aristocratic Laurenzano family, for whom he painted *The Adoration of the Shepherds*. This radiant Madonna and Child are exceptionally tender reminders of the Nativity.

Place stamps here

Place stamp here

Place stamp here

Contemporary Holiday

OCTOBER 9, NORTH POLE, ALASKA

Holiday Celebration (Hanukkah)

OCTOBER 22, WASHINGTON, DC

Traditional Holiday (Christmas)

NOVEMBER 1, RICHMOND, VIRGINIA

*S*o the light here kindled hath shown unto many . . . .

—WILLIAM BRADFORD, OF PLYMOUTH PLANTATION

The month of December is filled with important holidays.

This year, a special stamp has been designed in honor of Hanukkah, a Jewish celebration commemorating the rededication of the Second Temple of Jerusalem in 165 B.C., after its desecration three years earlier. Only enough oil to light the Temple menorah, or candelabrum, for one day was found, but the flame miraculously continued to burn for eight days. Today, several rituals mark the observation of Hanukkah: Families light a menorah for eight nights, exchange gifts, sing, play a game with a spinning top called a dreidel, and eat potato pancakes. Because Hanukkah centers around the miracle of light, candles are the primary symbol of the holiday. The artist, Hannah Smotrich, used colored cut paper to create the image for this year's Hanukkah stamp.

This year's block of four contemporary holiday stamps celebrates family, sharing, and the winter season as seen through the eyes of a New Englander. Illustrated by Julia Talcott, an artist based in Boston, the stamps depict the joy of the family hearth, shopping for gifts, and seasonal decorating.

The traditional holiday stamp for 1996 shows a detail from *The Adoration of the Shepherds*, painted in 1712 by Italian artist Paolo de Matteis. Considered a masterpiece, *The Adoration of the Shepherds* was painted for one of the leading contemporary patrons of art, the Duchess of Laurenzano. Now housed at the Virginia Museum of Fine Arts in Richmond, it typifies the late baroque or early rococo style of Naples.

This page (clockwise from top): colonial winter scene; North African Hanukkah lamp; Saint Vitus Cathedral, Prague; a toy truck; Christmas tree ornament. Opposite page: manuscript illustration of a menorah at Lisbon's Biblioteca Nacional. Inset: Raphael's Madonna del Granduca, Florence.

Place
stamps
here

The U.S. Postal Service is sponsoring an international professional cycling team, which hopes to compete in the 1997 Tour de France. Individual members also hope to be placed on the Olympic teams from their respective countries of origin. The Postal Service's squad will be led by Andy Hampsten, one of America's greatest cyclists. Rebecca Twigg, America's brightest hope for an Olympic cycling medal, is also a member of the team. Other members include Darren Baker, Dariusz Baranowski, Tomasz Brozyna, Michael Engleman, Chad Gerlach, Eddy Gragus, Tyler Hamilton, Phyllis Hines, Marty Jemison, Remigijus Lupeikis, Nate Reiss, Clark Sheehan, and Sven Teutenberg.

Cycling

I never felt so proud to be an American before, and indeed, I felt even more American at that moment than I had ever felt in America.

—MARSHALL "MAJOR" TAYLOR, ON WINNING THE MILE RACE
AT THE WORLD CHAMPIONSHIPS, MONTREAL, 1899

A sketch found in one of Leonardo da Vinci's notebooks shows something remarkably similar to the modern bicycle. Surely he would be amazed at the level of international popularity enjoyed by sport cycling today.

A 1,200-meter race in a park near Paris on May 31, 1868, marked the official beginning of organized sport cycling. The first race in England was held the following day. Town-to-town races and races staged over several days were established soon after. Roads on the European continent tended to be in better condition than those in England, where racing on tracks became more common. Racing began in the United States in 1878. America's greatest cyclists range from Marshall "Major" Taylor, a black rider who won international fame at the turn of the century, to Greg LeMond today.

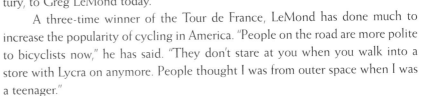

A three-time winner of the Tour de France, LeMond has done much to increase the popularity of cycling in America. "People on the road are more polite to bicyclists now," he has said. "They don't stare at you when you walk into a store with Lycra on anymore. People thought I was from outer space when I was a teenager."

Since it was established in 1903, the Tour de France has become the world's most prestigious cycling event. This annual race stretches over three weeks and covers more than 2,000 miles (3,220 kilometers) of both flat and mountainous terrain. Concentrated mostly in France and Belgium, the course also visits Spain, Italy, Germany, and Switzerland. Besides LeMond, other multiple winners of the Tour de France include Jacques Anquetil, of France, Eddy Merckx, of Belgium, Bernard Hinault, of France, and Miguel Indurain, of Spain, each of whom has won five times; and Jeannie Longo, a French rider who has won the women's Tour de France four times.

This page (clockwise from top middle): Marshall "Major" Taylor beginning a race in Berlin, 1901; U.S. Postal Service cycling team member Phyllis Hines; cyclists in motion during the 1995 Tour DuPont; cyclists racing in the 1995 Tour DuPont, including U.S. Postal Service team member Darren Baker, at left. Background: sketch found in one of Leonardo da Vinci's notebooks, circa 1500. Opposite page: Greg LeMond competing in the 1992 Tour de France. Inset: U.S. Postal Service cycling team member Nate Reiss getting water during the 1996 Tour DuPont.

PHOTO CREDITS

GEORGIA O'KEEFFE

Page 26
Alfred Stieglitz, *Georgia O'Keeffe*, The Beinecke Rare Book and Manuscript Library, Yale University Library; (inset) Georgia O'Keeffe, *From the Faraway Nearby*, 1937/The Metropolitan Museum of Art, Alfred Stieglitz Collection, 1959. (59.204.2)

Page 27
(clockwise from top) Laura Gilpin, *Georgia O'Keeffe Residence, May/June 1960*, safety negative, 1960, P1979.208.1876 (AR 4407.14)/ © 1981 Laura Gilpin Collection, Amon Carter Museum, Fort Worth, Texas; © Myron; Laura Gilpin, *Georgia O'Keeffe*, safety negative, 1953, P1979.230.4297 (O'Keeffe.13)/ © 1981 Laura Gilpin Collection, Amon Carter Museum, Fort Worth, Texas.

TENNESSEE STATEHOOD

Page 28
G. Ryan and S. Beyer/ Tony Stone; (inset) Tennessee State Library and Archives.

Page 29
(clockwise from top) © Dennis Thompson/ Unicorn Stock Photos; © Steve Davis; © Robin Hood; Jean Higgins/ Unicorn Stock Photos; Jean Higgins/ Unicorn Stock Photos; Charles E. Schmidt/ Unicorn Stock Photos.

AMERICAN INDIAN DANCES

Page 30
Jan Lucie; (inset) J. J. Foxx.

Page 31
(clockwise from top middle) Theo Westenburger/ Gamma Liaison; Hiroji Kubota/ Magnum Photos, Inc.; courtesy Nathan P. Jackson; Adam Woolfitt/Woodfin Camp & Associates, Inc.; © David Neel.

PREHISTORIC ANIMALS

Page 32
© Smithsonian Institution; (inset) negative #35273, courtesy Department of Library Services, American Museum of Natural History.

Page 33
(clockwise from top) © Shelly Grossman/ Woodfin Camp & Associates, Inc.; © John Gurche; © Lisa Biganzoli/ National Geographic Society Image Collection; Field Museum, transparency #CK8T; Smithsonian Institution.

BREAST CANCER AWARENESS

Page 34
© Lynn Johnson/Aurora.

Page 35
(clockwise from top) David A. White/Light Sources Stock; Kahn; © James Wilson/Woodfin Camp & Associates, Inc.; Kahn.

JAMES DEAN

Page 36
© Phil Stern photo; (inset) Floyd McCarty/Motion Picture and Television Photo Archive.

Page 37
(clockwise from top) Dennis Stock/Magnum Photos, Inc.; Photofest; Dennis Stock/ Magnum Photos, Inc.; Photofest.

FOLK HEROES

Page 38
(clockwise from top right) illustration from *Big Men, Big Country: A Collection of American Tall Tales* by Paul Robert Walker, illustrations © 1993 by John Bernardin, reproduced by permission of Harcourt Brace & Company; Library of Congress; illustration from *Here's Audacity!* by Frank Shay, illustration by Eben Given, published by Books for Libraries Press, Inc., New York, 1930; Palmer C. Hayden, *Hammer in His Hand*, Museum of African American Art, Los Angeles; (inset) Division of Rare and Manuscript Collections, Cornell University Library.

Page 39
(clockwise from top) Chesapeake and Ohio Historical Society, Clifton Forge, Virginia; West of the Pecos Museum, Pecos, Texas; National Baseball Library & Archive, Cooperstown, New York.

OLYMPIC ANNIVERSARY SHEET

Page 40
David Madison; (inset) Allsport/ IOC.

Page 41
(clockwise from top) IOC Archives; IOC Archives; Scala/Art Resource, New York; David Madison; (background) Scala/Art Resource, New York.

IOWA STATEHOOD

Page 42
Tom Till Photography; (inset) Putnam Museum of History and Natural Science, Davenport, Iowa.

Page 43
(clockwise from top) Andre Jenny/ Unicorn Stock Photos; Tom Bean; © Tom Raymond/ Tony Stone Images; John F. Schultz; Les Van/ Unicorn Stock Photos.

RURAL FREE DELIVERY

Page 44
Library of Congress; (inset) Erwin E. Smith, *Cowboy Mailing a Letter*, 1 C-S59-106; Erwin E. Smith Collection, Amon Carter Museum, Fort Worth, Texas.

Page 45
(clockwise from top) National Archives; Smithsonian Institution Libraries; National Postal Museum, Smithsonian Institution; National Archives.

PHOTO CREDITS

RIVERBOATS

Page 46
courtesy the Smithsonian Institution, National Museum of American History/ Transportation; (inset) Mariners' Museum.

Page 47
(clockwise from top) Steamboat Masters & Associates, Inc., Louisville, Kentucky; Warshaw Collection, Archives Center, National Museum of American History, Smithsonian Institution; courtesy Montana Historical Society; Steamboat Masters & Associates, Inc., Louisville, Kentucky.

BIG BAND LEADERS

Page 48
UPI/ Corbis-Bettmann; (inset) Archive Photos.

Page 49
(clockwise from top) Licensed by the heirs of Glenn Miller. Represented by CMG Worldwide, Inc., Indianapolis, Indiana. © Herb Snitzer/ Michael Ochs Archives; courtesy Michael Ochs Archives; Archive Photos/ John Leifert Collection; courtesy Michael Ochs Archives; Bettmann Archive.

SONGWRITERS

Page 50
Culver Pictures; (inset) UPI/ Corbis-Bettmann.

Page 51
(clockwise from top) UPI/Corbis-Bettmann; Archive Photos/ John Liefert Collection; UPI/Corbis-Bettmann; Culver Pictures.

F. SCOTT FITZGERALD

Page 52
Bettmann Archive; (inset) Bruccoli Collection, Thomas Cooper Library, University of South Carolina— photograph by George Fulton/ National Photography Network.

Page 53
(clockwise from top) Culver Pictures; Bruccoli Collection, Thomas Cooper Library, University of South Carolina— photograph by George Fulton/ National Photography Network; Photofest/Jagarts; Culver Pictures.

ENDANGERED SPECIES

Page 54
Robert Rattner; (inset) Frans Lanting/Minden Pictures.

Page 55
(clockwise from top middle) Ken Cole/Animals Animals; Jeff Vanuga; Thomas C. Emmel; Wendy Shattil/ Bob Rozinski; Joe McDonald/ Animals Animals.

COMPUTER TECHNOLOGY

Page 56
image provided by © 1994 PhotoDisc, Inc.; (inset) Smithsonian Institution.

Page 57
(clockwise from top) NCSA/University of Illinois at Urbana–Champaign; © Smithsonian Institution; © R. Grandadam/ Sygma; © Brooks Kraft/ Sygma; © William McCoy/ Rainbow.

CONTEMPORARY HOLIDAY, HOLIDAY CELEBRATION (HANUKKAH), TRADITIONAL HOLIDAY (CHRISTMAS)

Page 58
Giraudon/ Art Resource, New York; (inset) Raphael, *Madonna del Granduca*, Alinari/Art Resource, New York.

Page 59
(clockwise from top) *Poestenkill, New York: Winter*, © Abby Aldrich Rockefeller Folk Art Center, Williamsburg, Virginia; Geoffrey Clements, Jewish Museum/ Art Resource, New York; Catherine Carnow/Woodfin Camp & Associates, Inc.; image provided by © 1996 PhotoDisc, Inc.; Gary Hunter/ Tony Stone Images.

CYCLING

Page 60
© Yann Guichaoua/ Allsport/Agence Vandystadt; (inset) Mike Powell/Allsport.

Page 61
(clockwise from top middle) courtesy Indiana State Museum; © Casey B. Gibson, 1996; © Mike Powell/ Allsport; © Casey B. Gibson, 1996; (background) from *The American Bicycle* by Jay Pridmore and Jim Hurd, Motorbooks International, Osceola, Wisconsin, 1995.

These stamps and this stamp collecting book were produced by Stamp Services, United States Postal Service, Marvin Runyon, Postmaster General and Chief Executive Officer; Loren E. Smith, Chief Marketing Officer and Senior Vice President; Azeezaly S. Jaffer, Manager, Stamp Services.

Special thanks to the Stamp Services team and for key contributions by: Kathy Miller for project management; Paul Ovchinnikoff for print supervision; Wanda Parks for contract administration.

Visual and historical research: PhotoAssist, Inc. Artistic direction, design, and writing: Supon Design Group.